Macaws as Pets

A Complete Macaw Guide

Macaw Parrot Facts & Information, where to buy, health, diet, lifespan, types, breeding, fun facts and more!

By Lolly Brown

Foreword

Macaws has a history that dates back to as early as 17th Century, they have been kept as pets for a very long time and was even associated with a person's morality as well as religious significance during ancient times.

Macaw parrots were admired by bird enthusiasts mainly for their gorgeous colorful feathers and undeniable invigorating attitude. Some people say that they are a force to be reckoned with because they are larger than life! What a statement right?

Although Macaws are truly a great choice as pets, these birds doesn't come with a thin instruction manual, but fear not! In this book you'll be easily guided on understanding your Macaw pet, their behaviors, their characteristics, how you should feed and care for them and a whole lot more.

Embark on a wonderful journey of sharing your life with a Macaw Parrot. Learn to maximize the great privilege of living with one and be able to share this unique and unforgettable experience just like your ancestors that came before you!

Table of Contents

Chapter One: Introduction

Macaws are known as the "dream birds," not only because of their brilliant crafted colors but also because of their larger-than-life personalities.

These birds are considered as the giants of the parrot world, that's why they will definitely bring out the best in you and will surely serve you a purpose. They also have a reputation of being witty and loud yet sociable and loving at the same time.

They are recognized in six distinct genus; these are *Anodorhynchus, Cyanopsitta, Ara, Orthopsittaca, Primolius and Diopsittaca* with over 19 types or subspecies. Later on in this book, you will learn more about the different types of macaw parrots so that you can choose what is best for you!

Macaws are great as pets, though sometimes some people may find their attitudes very intimidating, but that's of course, part of who they are. They are clever and can be easily trained like any other birds, although, macaws are generally easy to care for, you will still need some useful tips, since these birds could potentially be harder to maintain than other kinds of parrots because of their huge sizes.

Macaw Parrots definitely lasts a lifetime! These birds have a lifespan of over 60 years! Now that's for keeps!

They're great longtime companions, and because of that you need some guidance on how to take care of them, raise them and possibly learn how to be like them as well as teach them to be like you!!

Fortunately, this ultimate guide will teach you on how to be the best Macaw owner you can be! Inside this book, you will find tons of helpful information about Macaw Parrots: how they live, how to deal with them and realize the great benefits of owning one!

Glossary of Important Terms

Archaeological – a scientific study of material remains (such as fossil relics and artifacts of human or animal species)

Avian – Pertaining to birds.

Asymptomatic – having or showing no symptoms of disease

Beak – The mouth of a bird consisting of the upper and lower mandibles.

Breast – The chest of a bird located between the chin and the abdomen.

Breeding – an act of producing young animals

Brood – a group of young birds all born at the same time.

Chick – A newly hatched bird; a baby bird.

Clutch – The eggs laid by a female bird in a single setting.

Cuttlebone – the shell of a cuttlefish that is used for supplying cage birds with lime and salts.

Flock – A group of birds.

Fossils – reserved from a past geologic age

Hatching – The process through which baby birds emerge from the egg.

Hatchling - A newly hatched chick.

Hybrid – a macaw that is produced by combining two different kinds of species.

Incubation – The act or process of keeping eggs warm which causes it to eventually hatch.

Nares – the openings of the bird's nose or nasal cavity.

Nape – back of the neck

Pinfeathers – a not fully developed feather emerging from the skin

Plumage – the feathers that cover the body of the bird

Sexual Dimorphism – Referring to physical differences between the sexes of the same species.

Suppler – ability to bent or twist easily

Stargazing – a twisted back in birds.

Taxonomy – The classification of species into order, family, genera, etc.

Tetra-Chromic – four color light vision including ultraviolet.

Urates – a salt of uric acid.

UVA – a radiation that causes tanning of the skin.

UVB – a radiation that is responsible for sunburn in the skin.

Wingspan – distance from the tip of one wing of a bird to the tip of the other wing.

Chapter Two: Meet Macaws

The great thing about Macaws is that they are BIG IN SIZE AND INSIDE! Before getting a beautifully crafted bird as your pet, it's very important that you know what it is inside out! Like many other things, you need to have proper knowledge and invest a significant amount of time to truly study and understand where these birds are coming from. That is how you will determine if this kind of pet is the right choice, so that you know what you are dealing with.

On the next page, you'll be introduced to one of the most respected parrots in the world. Prepare to meet macaws!

What are Macaws?

Macaws, which are scientifically under the Subfamily of *Arinae*, are birds that are native to Mexico, Central America, South America, and formerly the Caribbean. These birds can live up to possibly over 60 years!

They look intimidating at first and can be quite tough sometimes, but inside they are soft and sensitive creatures which make them an interesting choice as pets.

These parrots had been popular since the turn of the 17th century and because of their brilliantly colored feathers they were associated with some religious significance and highly adored by Pueblo Indians in United States.

Macaws are mostly large in size but there are also other types which are relatively small. They have vivid colorful feathers that come in an array of different colors like yellow, green, blue, white and red. Different variations of hybrid macaws also exist, mainly for pet trade.

Macaw parrots have about 23 subspecies, classified into 6 types or genera; these are *Anodorhynchus, Cyanopsitta, Ara, Orthopsittaca, Primolius and Diopsittaca.*

Since these birds are quite large, that usually means that they have loud voices and love to screech a lot, but they can be quickly taught to speak, whistle and imitate other sounds like most birds in general.

Aside from talking, they are also fond of chewing and playing challenging games to exercise their intelligence. Sometimes what they do is intimidate people by leaning towards them just to see the startled look on their faces and reaction! Yes, they are totally witty and have a knack for a fun time!

Most Macaws are generally easy to train and can be well-behaved as long as you provide them with adequate attention, interaction, and love. They can easily become part of the family and a loving companion if you are willing to put in the time and effort to take care of them.

Facts about Macaws

Macaws can be easily identified because they have slim bodies, quite broad heads, very long pointed tails and wings that allow them to swiftly fly as well as powerful sharp beaks, which ultimately gain them some degree of respect among the parrot species.

Their average size including tails is about 11 – 39 inches, with a wingspan of 86 – 140 cm, a top speed of 24km/h and weighs about 907 – 1814 grams. It has an average lifespan of 50 – 60 years.

In terms of their behavior and personality, they are quite notorious for having a difficult attitude, their sharp beaks and jaws can be used for biting, feather-plucking and screaming. Due to their intelligence and curious minds, they tend to chew on any objects available and require lots of interaction.

These parrots are omnivorous and usually feed on seeds, insects, fruit and nuts. Macaws are not sexually dimorphic; although males can be identified by their larger heads than females. DNA sexing is highly recommended to determine the gender of a macaw parrot.

In terms of reproduction, the ideal breeding age starts at 4 to 8 years old; females' clutch size ranges from 2 – 3 eggs and incubation lasts for about 22 – 24 days.

Majority of these birds are endangered species in the wild. Some macaws species are now extinct such as the Spix's Macaw and Cuban Red Macaw due to bird smuggle.

These birds can be trained to mimic human speech and imitate other sounds by using their bifurcated trachea, which are equivalent to vocal cords in humans.

Quick Facts

- **Taxonomy**: phylum *Chordata*, class *Aves*, order *Psittaciformes*, family *Psittacidae*, Subfamily *Arinae*, Tribe *Arini.*
- **Distribution**: Mexico, Central and South America
- **Habitat**: Tropical Rainforests, Palm Swamp Forests
- **Lifestyle**: Flock Oriented
- **Anatomical Adaptations**:
- **Breeding Season**: February – June
- **Eggs**: 2 – 3 eggs
- **Incubation Period**: 26 - 28 days
- **Average Size**: 30cm - 100cm (11.8 to 39.5 in)
- **Average Weight**: 907grams - 1814 grams
- **Wingspan**: 86cm - 140cm (34in - 56in)
- **Top Speed:** 24km/h (15mph)
- **Coloration**: yellow, green, blue, white, red
- **Sexual Dimorphism**: Cannot be determine by physical characteristics; needs DNA testing
- **Conservation Status:** Endangered
- **Diet**: Seeds, Insects, Fruit, Nuts (Omnivore)
- **Sounds:** Vocal Communicator
- **Interaction:** Highly Social
- **Lifespan**: 50 - 60 years

Macaws in History

There had been historical records of Macaws since 1100 A.D. Some records also indicate that a Green-Winged Macaw was prominent and had been around earlier than 17th century.

In 1536, Pueblo Indians living in United States (around the area of New Mexico and Arizona today), are trading parrot's feathers for green stones in the north, according to Lyndon Hargrove in his notes written in 1970.

In 1716, Padre Velarde, a Spanish priest, saw some Pima Indians raising a bird for their colorful feathers and adornment. As mentioned earlier, the Indians' religious practice associated the color of the feathers with a person's morality, suggesting that if you cannot keep a red-colored Macaw then you have a poor moral character.

During the 20th century, macaws were already prominent and kept as pets in Europe and United States especially during the 1900s. However, due to the two World Wars and bird diseases outbreaks, the number of parrot species decline.

Today, bird importation is still restricted but many macaw species are successfully bred in captivity and readily available in local pet stores and avian breeders.

Types of Macaws

Macaws aren't just huge birds; they also came from a huge family! There are about 19 known species of macaws belonging to 6 main categories or types.

In this section, you will learn all of the different kinds of macaws, their major characteristics, their colors as well as their conservation status because some of them are highly endangered and even extinct already, obviously if they are, then you won't be able to acquire these types of birds but the great thing is that, there are lots to choose from. Read on!

Here is a quick overview of the 6 categories with over

23 species of Macaws in order.

4.1.) Genus *Anodorhynchus*

Common Name	Scientific Name
• Glaucous macaw	Anodorhynchus Glaucus
• Hyacinth macaw	Anodorhynchus Hyacinthinus
• Lear's macaw	Anodorhynchus Leari

4.2.) Genus *Cyanopsitta*

Common Name	Scientific Name
• Spix's macaw	Cyanopsitta Spixii

4.3) Genus *Ara*

Common Name	Scientific Name
• Blue-and-yellow macaw	Ara Ararauna
• Blue-throated macaw	Ara Glaucogularis
• Military Macaw	Ara Militaris

• Buffon's Macaw	Ara Ambiguus
• Scarlet macaw	Ara Macao
• Green-winged macaw	Ara Chloroptera
• Red-fronted macaw	Ara Rubrogenys
• Chestnut-fronted macaw	Ara Severa
• Dominican green-and-yellow macaw	Ara Atwoodi
• Jamaican green-and-yellow macaw	Ara Erythrocephala
• Jamaican red macaw	Ara Gossei
• Lesser Antillean macaw	Ara Guadeloupensis
• Cuban red macaw	Ara Tricolor
• Saint Croix macaw	Ara Autocthones

4.4) Genus *Orthopsittaca*

Common Name	Scientific Name
• Red-bellied macaw	Orthopsittaca Manilata

4.5) Genus *Primolius*

Common Name	Scientific Name
• Blue-headed macaw	Primolius Couloni
• Blue-winged macaw	Primolius Maracana
• Golden-collared macaw	Primolius Auricollis

4.6) Genus *Diopsittaca*

Common Name	Scientific Name
• Red-shouldered macaw	Diopsittaca Nobilis

Genus Anodorhynchus

Anodorhynchus is composed of large blue macaws species found in central and eastern South America that usually inhabits an open and semi-open areas. This genus includes three species, one of which is already extinct.

a.) Glaucous Macaw

It has a turquoise-blue body color with a greyish head. Its size is about 75 cm and has a wingspan of 85 – 95 cm. This species was last recorded in the 1870s; due to extreme smuggling of birds as well as loss of palm-forests they eventually became extinct. These birds are native in north Argentina and south Paraguay.

Quick Facts:
Size: 65 – 75 cm
Wingspan: 85 – 95 cm
Life Span: 14 – 60 years
Body Color: Turquoise-blue
Conservation Status: Extinct

b.) Hyacinth Macaw

These birds are known as the largest and longest kind of parrot in the world! Despite of their huge size, they are reputable for being the calmest of all parrot species; these birds are often referred to as the "gentle giants."
Hyacinth macaws are native to focal South America.

Although these species are also declining in population, they can still be found in Brazil, Paraguay and Bolivia.

Hyacinths can be excellent pets, but like any other parrots, the owner needs to have a broad knowledge on how to take care of such species. Their beaks are extremely sharp and strong which could harm people if not trained properly. These parrots love human interaction and are also extremely intelligent creatures.

Quick Facts:
Size: about 100 cm
Weight: 1179 grams – 1678 grams
Wingspan: about 120 cm
Life Span: 50 – 60 years
Body Color: Bright Blue
Conservation Status: Threated with Extinction (Appendix I)

c.) Lear's macaw

These parrots are also known as Indigo Macaw, they are native to Brazil and measures about 70 – 75 cm, weighing about 950 grams with a wingspan of about 100 cm and a lifespan of 30 -50 years. Its top flight speed is about 35 miles per hour.

Its body color is metallic blue and has a patch of yellow skin adjacent to its bill. It is also describe as slightly smaller Glaucous and a larger Hyacinth Macaw.

These birds are extremely rare and have a very limited range. Today Lear's macaw currently have a population of about 1200 – 1300, however they are still considered as an endangered species due to rampant hunting and bird trade.

Quick Facts:
Size: 70 – 75 cm
Weight: 950 grams
Wingspan: about 100 cm
Life Span: 30 - 50 years
Body Color: Dark, Metallic Blue
Conservation Status: Threated with Extinction (Appendix I)

Genus Cyanopsitta

This genus has only one specie; unfortunately this bird is already extinct. It is the Spix's macaw.

a.) Spix's macaw

These parrots are said to be native in Brazil, they are measure 22 inches from head to tail and has a wingspan of approximately 10-11 inches. These parrots are mostly blue in body color and have a shade of grey in its head area.

Its population was already declining during 1819 and due to continuous deforestation, smuggling, illegal logging and several land development, these birds completely became extinct in the 1970's.

Quick Facts:
Size: 22 inches
Wingspan: 10 -11 inches
Body Color: Blue
Conservation Status: Extinct

Genus Ara

The Ara genus has 10 macaw species, two of which are already extinct. They are described by experts as large neo-tropical birds with long tails and bright colored plumages that distinctively look alike with the male and female species.

a.) Blue-and-Yellow Macaw

These birds are also known as blue-and-gold macaw, mainly because of their body colors. They are native to South America and they inhabit woodlands and swamp forests. They are one of the largest members of the macaw family; it measures about 30 - 34 inches and weighs about 900 - 1100 grams, it has a wingspan of 41 - 45 inches and can live up to 80 years!

These birds have an extensive range in South America and Central America, particularly in Bolivia, Peru, Brazil, Panama, Ecuador, Venezuela and Paraguay. Blue-and-yellow macaws are not highly endangered animals and can be great as pets.

Quick Facts:

Size: 30 -34 inches

Weight: 900 – 1100 grams

Wingspan: 41-45 inches

Life Span: 80 years

Body Color: Blue and Gold/Yellow

Conservation Status: Not necessarily threatened with Extinction (Appendix II)

b.) Blue-Throated Macaw

These birds are commonly known as *Wagler's Macaw* as well as *Caninde Macaw*. They are mostly found in northern Bolivia and mostly inhabit savannah grasslands and swamps.

These birds measures about 34 inches from head to tail and weighs approximately 750 grams with a lifespan of about 80 years. Its throat and cheeks are all blue even its under tail. Its wings and plumage is usually turquoise colored. Some experts believed that it is a subspecies of blue-and-yellow macaw because of its similarities. Blue-throated macaws are highly endangered due to their small population and as a result of illegal bird trade.

Quick Facts:

Size: 34 inches

Weight: 750 grams

Life Span: 80 years

Body Color: Blue; Turquoise

Conservation Status: Threated with Extinction (Appendix I)

c.) Military Macaw

Their body color, which is "military" green, is the main reason on how they got their name and because it resembles a military uniform. These birds are native to South America and usually inhabit forests particularly in Mexico. Generally these macaws measure about 33-43 inches, has a wingspan of 39 - 43 inches, weighs about 862- 1200 grams and can live up to 60 years in the wild.

One interesting fact about them is that their personality enters the room before they do! According to bird enthusiasts, they love to shriek and are usually very noisy; however, like other types of macaws, they are very interactive and sociable as well. Keep that in mind before buying one!

Quick Facts:

Size: 33-43 inches

Weight: 862- 1200 grams

Wingspan: 39 – 43 inches

Life Span: 60 years

Body Color: Darkish Green

Conservation Status: Threated with Extinction (Appendix I)

d.) Buffon's Macaw

The Buffon's macaw, also known as Great Green Macaw, is usually confused with the Military Macaw because of its similar body colors.

These bird measures about 33 - 35 inches, weighs about 1300 grams and has a wingspan of 50 inches. They are endemic in Ecuador and have a large population in South America particularly in the wet lowlands of Honduras. Their body color is mostly green with a distinctive reddish forehead and bluish-green plumage and feathers.

Quick Facts:

Size: 33-35 inches

Weight: 1300 grams

Wingspan: 50 inches

Body Color: Green

Conservation Status: Threated with Extinction (Appendix I)

e.) Scarlet Macaw

Scarlet Macaw is the National Bird of Honduras. These birds are endemic in humid forests of Bolivia, Columbia, Peru, Brazil and Mexico. It measures about 32-36 inches from head to tip of the tail, weighs about 1000 grams and has a wingspan of 1 meter. Typically these birds can live up to 50 years in the wild and 75 years in captivity. It has scarlet plumage with touch of blue and yellow, sometimes green upper wings.

An interesting fact about these macaws is that they have great vocalization, vision and hearing and bird enthusiasts consider them as one of the most magnificent macaw species. These birds are not endangered but are highly threatened by illegal trading.

Quick Facts:

Size: 32 -36 inches

Weight: 1000 grams

Wingspan: 1 meter

Lifespan: 50 -75 years

Body Color: Scarlet

Conservation Status: Not necessarily threatened with Extinction (Appendix II)

f.) Green-Winged Macaw

These birds are often confused with Scarlet Macaw because of similar body and feather colors.

These birds measure about 35.5 inches, with an average wingspan of 41-49 inches and weighing approximately 1250 - 1700 grams that has a lifespan of 60 years and more. Like the Hyacinth Macaws, they are also considered as "gentle giants." They are very ideal as pets because of their sweet nature and sociable characteristics.

They are not endangered but vulnerable to extinction because of deforestation and other illegal human activities that affect these birds' habitats. They can be usually found in savannahs and swamps of South America particularly in French Guiana, Ecuador, Peru, Brazil, Bolivia and Paraguay.

Quick Facts:

Size: 35.5 inches

Weight: 1250 - 1700 grams

Wingspan: 41-49 inches

Lifespan: 60 years

Body Color: Green

Conservation Status: Not necessarily threatened with Extinction (Appendix II)

g.) Red-Fronted Macaw

These birds are found in semi-desert mountain areas of Bolivia that has a semi-arid climate. Its body color is green with a reddish forehead and patch of red over the ears and wings. It measures about 21 - 23 inches long, a wingspan of 80 -86 cm and weighs about 500-600 grams. Its life expectancy is 25 - 50 years.

These birds are highly endangered and also vulnerable to pet trading.

Quick Facts:

Size: 21 - 23 inches

Weight: 500-600 grams

Wingspan: 80 -86 cm

Lifespan: 25 - 50 years

Body Color: Green with reddish forehead

Conservation Status: Threated with Extinction (Appendix I)

h.) Chestnut-Fronted Macaw

These birds are also known as Severe Macaw; they are one of the smaller types of macaws that's why they are also sometimes referred to as the "mini-macaws" because it only measures about 18 inches from head to tail. Their foreheads have a brown chestnut patch, hence the name.

Their body color is green, with a touch of red and blue on its wings and plumage. It weighs about 300-400 grams that has a lifespan of 45-50 years. It is endemic in Amazonian Brazil and Bolivia. These birds are not endangered, although vulnerable to pet trading. They interestingly like to be held and pet, unlike other birds and are also highly sociable. They can be great choice as pets.

Quick Facts:

Size: 18 inches

Weight: 300-400 grams

Lifespan: 45-50 years

Body Color: Green with brown chestnut patch

Conservation Status: Not necessarily threatened with Extinction (Appendix II)

i.) Dominican Green-and-Yellow Macaw

These birds are also known as Atwood's Macaw or simply Dominican Macaw. This macaw is believed to be extinct in the late 19th century and was hypothetically native in the Island of Dominica. However, there was no actual proof and archeological confirmation of this bird's existence; it was only described and was believed to be seen by a scientist and zoologist, Dr. Thomas Atwood, hence the name.

Quick Facts:

Size/Weight: Unknown

Body Color: Hypothetically Green and Yellow

Conservation Status: Hypothetically Extinct

j.) Jamaican Green-and-Yellow Macaw

This bird was also extinct since the 19th century and was native to forests and mountains in Jamaica. According to the notes of a scientist named, Gosse, he described its body color as green with reddish head, and also has a yellowish tail and wings. These parrots are also considered as hypothetically extinct because no archaeological remains were found that may prove its existence.

Quick Facts:
Size/Weight: Unknown
Body Color: Hypothetically Green body and Yellowish tail
Conservation Status: Hypothetically Extinct

k.) Jamaican Red Macaw

This macaw is also potentially extinct; it was believed to be discovered by Dr. Robertson in 1765 in Jamaica. Its body is primarily red in color with yellowish shred of color from the top of its head down to the nape of the neck with bluish under wings.

Quick Facts:
Size/Weight: Unknown
Body Color: Hypothetically Red body and Bluish wings
Conservation Status: Hypothetically Extinct

l.) Lesser Antillean macaw

These parrots are also known as Guadeloupe Macaw, because this specie was found and native in the island of Guadeloupe around the Atlantic Ocean. It measures about 15 – 20 inches and weighs approximately 1500 grams. It has a red body color and tail with yellowish-blue wings. Its extinction is due to an outbreak of disease and hunting by humans.

Quick Facts:

Size: 15 – 20 inches

Weight: 1500 grams

Body Color: Red

Conservation Status: Extinct

m.) Cuban Macaw

These macaws had been extinct in the late 19th Century due to human activities such as hunting and trading. They were native in Cuba and according to experts they inhabited swamps and open terrains. It has an orange-colored forehead and yellowish nape, reddish-brown feathers and blue plumage. It is also one of the mini - macaws which is only 20 inches in length and a wingspan of about 290 mm.

Quick Facts:

Size: 20 inches

Wingspan: 290 mm

Body Color: Yellowish Nape, Reddish-brown feathers

Conservation Status: Extinct

n.) Saint Croix Macaw

Scientists found fossils of these parrots during the 1930's. Saint Croix Macaws' bones dates back in around 300 C.E. although there weren't any proof yet on its exact timeline. They were native in Saint Croix and Puerto Rico in the Caribbean. It is believed to be slightly smaller than a Cuban Macaw.

Quick Facts:

Size: slightly smaller than Cuban Macaw
Conservation Status: Extinct

Genus Orthopsittaca

The Red-Bellied Macaw, which is scientifically known as *Orthopsittaca manilata* is the only known species under the Genus Orthopsittaca.

a.) Red-Bellied Macaw

These birds are also known as Guacamaya Manilata. Its name came from the maroon colored patch in its belly. It inhabits savannahs and swampy forests in South America particularly in Columbia, Brazil and Trinidad. These birds also prefer to live in palm-groves, they measure about 18 inches, weighs around 300 grams and has a life expectancy of 40 years.

They have mostly greenish body color, greyish

plumage, reddish belly and bluish, sometimes orange or yellow under wings. They are very noisy and love to be in flocks. These parrot's population is declining due to pet trade and loss of habitat because of palms and forests clearings.

Quick Facts:
Size: 18 inches
Weight: 300 grams
Lifespan: 40 years
Body Color: Green with red belly
Conservation Status: Not necessarily threatened with Extinction (Appendix II)

Genus Primolius

This genus is composed of 3 macaw species, which are also considered as mini-macaws. They are mostly green in body color with a touch of blue, yellow and red to its feathers and wings.

a.) Blue-Headed Macaw

These birds have an extensive range in lowlands of Peru and western Brazil. It measures about 16 inches, weighs about 207 - 300 grams. It has a bluish head and flight feathers, full green body color, yellowish plumage and according to bird enthusiasts it has an undeniably large and heavy bill more than any other medium-sized macaws. They are not endangered although highly susceptible to illegal trading like other macaws.

Quick Facts:

Size: 16 inches

Weight: 207 - 300 grams

Body Color: Green with bluish head and flight feathers

Conservation Status: Threated with Extinction (Appendix I)

b.) Blue-winged Macaw

This macaw is also known as the Illiger's macaw. It is endemic in decidous and evergreen forests of South America, particularly in Argentina, Bolivia, and Paraguay.

These birds have a pale green body color with a red patch on its chest and bluish under wings. It weighs about 265 grams, 43 cm in length with a lifespan of 50 - 60 years. It is nearly threatened according to CITES appendices.

As a pet, blue-winged macaws are loving and playful but are also loud and loves to screech a lot, so watch out for that!

Quick Facts:

Size: 43 cm

Weight: 265 grams

Lifespan: 50 - 60 years

Body Color: Pale Green with red patch and blue wings

Conservation Status: Threated with Extinction (Appendix I)

c.) Golden - Collared Macaw

These birds are also one of the mini-macaws; they are abundant in focal South America and inhabit woodlands, savannahs and lowlands especially in Argentina, Brazil and Paraguay. They are typically 15 inches in length, has a weight of approximately 250 -280 grams and can live up to 30-40 years.

They have mostly green body color, with a shred of yellow on their nape and bluish-maroon sometimes with a touch of yellow plumage as well as blackish forehead. These birds are marked as "least concerned" in CITES appendices and commercial trade is allowed provided that the sellers have an export permit. They are described as quite mischievous but very clever and love to be with a small flock.

Quick Facts:

Size: 15 inches

Weight: 250 -280 grams

Lifespan: 30-40 years.

Body Color: Green with shred of yellow and blackish forehead

Conservation Status: Not necessarily threatened with Extinction (Appendix II)

Genus Diopsittaca

The red-shouldered macaw, which is scientifically known as *Diopsittaca nobilis,* is the only known specie under Genus Diopsittaca. There are 2 types of Red-shouldered Macaw which is called the Noble Macaw and Hanh's Macaw

a.) Red-Shouldered Macaw

These neo-tropical parrots are considered as the smallest in the macaw family, they only measure about 12 inches and has a weight of 165 grams! Yes, you can literally carry them on your pocket - but please don't!

They have a full green body colored with a noticeable reddish patch on their shoulder and bluish feathers on their forehead. They have a reputation for being clever and nice macaws, although they are also fond of screeching just like other macaw parrots. Unfortunately due to human activities, their population is declining and trading of these macaws is listed as restricted for pet trading according to BirdLife International. In captivity these parrots can live up to 50 years! Now that's what you can count on for sure!

Quick Facts:

Size: 12 inches

Weight: 165 grams

Lifespan: 50 years.

Body Color: Green with red patch on shoulder

Conservation Status: Not necessarily threatened with Extinction (Appendix II)

Chapter Three: Macaws' Requirements

Are you now thinking of getting a Macaw? No problem! After learning what Macaws are, where they come from, how they live and its different types, it's time to give you practical tips on what you need to know before buying one.

In this chapter, you will get a whole lot of information on its pros and cons, its average monthly costs as well as the things you need so that you will be well on your way to becoming a legitimate Macaw pet owner -should you decide to be one! It's up to you! Read on!

Pros and Cons of Macaws

The information listed below are the advantages and disadvantages of owning Macaws:

Pros

- **Personality:** They are highly interactive, clever, resourceful and easy to get along with
- **Appearance:** Vibrant and vividly colorful
- **Speaking Ability:** They can be taught to speak and is also a quick learner
- **Impact on Humans:** These birds are a force to be reckoned with; they'll definitely bring out the best in you!

Cons

- **Damage to Your Home**: They love to chew up and destroy your wooden furniture if left out of the cage.
- **Behavior:** They are prone to feather-destructive behaviors or feather-plucking due to boredom.
- **Cost:** They can easily destroy toys; you may need to constantly buy new ones for them to play with.
- **Noise:** They are loud screamers and have ear-piercing screeches. Not advisable if you live in an apartment.

Macaws Behavior with other pets

There is actually no general rule when introducing your pet parrot with other types or species of birds, sometimes they'll get along, sometimes they won't. When it comes to Macaws, it is ideal to introduce your parrot with its own kind.

Macaws tend to get along well with other macaws, however, experts recommend great supervision is needed upon introduction especially for smaller bird macaw to avoid bullying. Otherwise it is wise to just separate them.

It is also best done if the macaws are still young,

because they are still vulnerable and can be very accepting of other members once they get used to it. Since they are quite large in size compare to other birds, it is also ideal to just own one for a while and then gradually buy more if you know how to manage them already.

You can also introduce other types of birds but do so with caution so that they could easily warm up with their new feathered friend.

Macaws love to travel and fly in flocks when they're in the wild but in captivity, like other birds, they are highly individual. Experts also suggest that the best behaved macaws are those who were exposed to lots of change in the environment and the ones who were trained to socialize with people, because they become more adjusted.

Ease and Cost of Care

Owning a Macaw doesn't come cheap! Aside from the fact that they are mostly large and could really be of high maintenance, these birds are also highly in demand because of their distinctively vivid colors and rarity, which makes them more expensive than other bird species, not to mention the supplies you'll need in order to maintain and keep one. These things will definitely add up to your daily life expenses. If you want to own a macaw as a pet you should be able to cover the necessary costs it entails.

In this section you will receive an overview of the expenses associated with purchasing and keeping a Macaw as a pet.

Initial Costs

The initial expenses associated with keeping Macaws as pets include the cost of the bird itself as well as the cage, cage accessories, toys, and grooming supplies.

You will find an overview of these costs below as well as the estimated total expense for keeping a Macaw:

Purchase Price: starts at $800 - $10,000

As mentioned earlier Macaws, even the smaller ones are very expensive. Mini-macaws usually has a starting price of $800 and larger macaws such as Green-winged, Military and Hyacinth most likely costs anywhere between $1500 - $10,000 sometimes even up to $18,000! The general rules in these birds are, the more colorful, rarer and clever it is, the more expensive it can be. So better check your budget to see which macaw is best for you.

Cage: starts at $400-$1000

The bigger the specie, the bigger the cage! It's a general rule for birds that they live in cages where they could have the luxury of space, after all that are where they're going to spend most of their time right? So pick the right cage for your macaw, so that they'll enjoy life like you!

Accessories: more or less $100 in total

If you bought a cage, you'll definitely need cage accessories like perches, lights, feeding dishes, stands, cage covers and harnesses for your Macaw. Accessories can be quite expensive depending on the brand as well as the quality and size of your purchase. Macaws are quite naughty birds, they'll chew everything! Watch out!

Toys: more or less $70

Macaws loves to chew things especially toys! They prefer bigger ones, which usually means more expensive for your budget, because according to bird enthusiasts and macaw owners macaws are addicted to destroying their toys in the shortest time possible! Like other parrots, they need plenty of stimulation to keep their intelligent and curious minds entertained. Keep birdie boredom at bay with chewable toys for your macaw.

Grooming Supplies: more or less $70 in total

As part of pet hygiene, your feathered friend needs to be cleaned and properly groomed. There are lots of grooming supplies that you can buy online or in your local pet store. Again, the brand and quality of the product affect the price range to keep your macaws clean and healthy.

Initial Cost for Macaws	
Cost Type	**Approximate Cost**
Purchase Price	$800 (£547.52)
Cage	$400 (£273.76)
Accessories	$100 (£89)
Toys	$70 (£47.91)
Grooming Supplies	$70 (£63)
Total	$1440 (£985.53)

*Please note that these amounts are computed at the starting price. Costs may vary.

Monthly Costs

The monthly costs associated with keeping a Macaw can be totally expensive! Some of the things that needs to be bought on a monthly basis like food supplements, cleaning materials, not to mention toys and even veterinary care every now and then will definitely add up to your expenses. Below are the estimate monthly costs it entails.

Bird Food (seeds, pellets, treats, fruits, vegetables, etc.): approximately $50-$70 per month

Your Macaws particularly have a more expensive bird food than other kinds of parrot. They need a variety of food to keep their diet healthy. There's a massive selection of high quality seed diets, complete food and pelleted foods to choose from both online and in your local pet stores, as mentioned before, the cost will depend on the brand, the quantity as well as the nutritional value of the food.

Feeding a variety of these foods, alongside fruits and vegetables is the key to a healthy parrot.

Cleaning Supplies: at least $10 per month

You don't need brand new cleaning supplies every month, but of course, you will run out of bird shampoo and soap eventually. Just include it in your budget.

Veterinary Care: starts at $150 - $1,000 or more

As mentioned earlier, Macaws are very prone to feather-plucking, that's why you may end up either buying more toys to keep them from doing that or take them to an avian vet for a medical check-up every now and then.

Avian vets are trained specifically to work with exotic birds whereas a general practicing vet may not be familiar with their needs and treatments especially if they are sick, not to mention the medicines needed. If in case, this happens it's better and wiser to set aside a portion of your budget for any medical needs that will come up.

Additional Costs: at least $10 per month

In addition to all of these monthly costs you should plan for occasional extra costs like repairs to your Macaw cage, replacement toys, food supplements, medicines etc. You won't have to cover these costs every month but you should include it in your budget to be safe.

Monthly Costs for Macaws	
Cost Type	**Approximate Cost**
Bird Food	$50 (£34.22)
Cleaning Supplies	$10 (£8)
Veterinary Care (optional)	$150 (£135)
Additional Costs	$10 (£8)
Total	$220 (£150.57)

*Please note that these amounts are computed at the starting price. Costs may vary.

Chapter Four: Tips in Buying Macaws

If you are still interested in reading this chapter, that only means one thing: you have already decided to buy a Macaw! Good choice, they are really cool and fun birds!

Here you will learn tips and tricks on how to select a healthy macaw, where to find the right breeder as well as the laws and permit you need to be aware of before buying.

Restrictions and Regulations in United States

If you are planning to acquire a Macaw as your pet, then you have to think beyond the cage. There are certain restrictions and regulations that you need to be aware of, because it will not only serve as protection for your bird but also for you. Here are some things you need to know regarding the acquirement of Macaws both in United States and in Great Britain.

a.) What is CITES?

CITES stands for Convention on International Trade in Endangered Species of Wild Fauna and Flora. It protects Macaws by regulating its import, export, and re-export through an international convention authorized through a licensing system.

It is also an international agreement, drafted by the International Union for Conservation of Nature (IUCN), which aims to ensure that the trade in specimens of wild animals and plants does not threaten their survival.

Different species are assigned in different appendix statuses such as Appendix I, II or III etc. These appendices indicate the level of threat to the current population of the bird with consideration to their likely ability to rebound in the wild with legal trade.

b.) Appendix I and II of CITES

Some macaws are considered potentially endangered or highly threatened as indicated in CITES' Appendix I while some are not (Appendix II). In this section, you'll learn what the differences between the two appendices are and how to get the permits necessary.

Appendix I simply means that birds or macaws in particular, that are on this list means that they are most or likely endangered species and may require import or export permit to prevent illegal trading.

If your macaw is in Appendix II, that means not necessarily now threatened with extinction but are still vulnerable. International trade may be granted an export permit or certificate and no import permit is required for the species listed in Appendix II, although some countries make require such permits for safety purposes. (Please refer to the conservation status and appendix number of each macaw specie on Chapter 2 of this book)

The Division of Management Authority processes applications for CITES permits for the United States. You should allow at least 60 days for the review of your permit applications.

For more information on how to apply for a CITES permit please visit their website at: <http://www.fws.gov/international/cites/>

Permit in Great Britain and Australia

In Great Britain and Australia you may need a permit for you to be able to import, export, or travel with your Macaw. This permit is called an **Animal Movement License.**

Aside from the CITES permit, sometimes a Pet Bird Import License and a veterinary health certificate are required before bringing your bird in Great Britain.

You can apply for a Pet Bird Import License through this link: <http://AHITchelmsford@animalhealth.gsi.gov.uk.>

Like in the United States being aware of the regulations and getting a license is an important thing you need to consider before you acquire, import or export a bird. This does not only protect the animals but it can also avoid confiscation of your pet.

Practical Tips in Buying Macaws

Now that you are already aware and have prior knowledge about the legal aspects of owning a macaw, the next step is purchasing one through a local pet store or a legitimate breeder.

Here are some recommendations for finding a reputable Macaw parrot breeders in United States and in Great Britain.

a.) How to Find a Macaw Breeder

The first thing you need to do is to look for a legit avian breeder or pet store in your area that specializes in Macaws.

You can also find great avian breeders online but you have to take into consideration the validity of the breeder. It is highly recommended that you see your new bird in person before buying anything on the internet. You can find several recommended list of Macaw breeder websites later in this book.

If possible, spend as much time as you can with your prospective new Macaw before buying it. Interact with the bird and see how it is with you.

Continue the diet of the bird as advised by the store owner or breeder to maintain its eating habits. Look for any health problems or issues as well.

Finally, only purchase a Macaw that is banded. Banding means the bird have a small metal band on one of its legs placed at birth by the breeder which is inscribed with the bird's clutch number, date of birth and the breeder number.

Leg bands are indicators that the purchaser and the bird itself are in the country legally and have not been smuggled.

b.) Local Macaw Breeders in the United States

Here are the lists of available Macaw breeders in the United States sorted by each species with its current rate.

Availability and costs of these macaws may vary over time, please check the links provided for any updates.

Blue and Gold Macaw Breeders

Birdmans Baby Parrots

5668 N Lincoln Ave Chicago, Illinois

Website: www.birdmansparrots.com

Tel. No.: 773-317-3785

Price: $1,800.00

The Bird Nerd

1818 Sanctuary Rd, Naples, Florida

Website: http://www.birdbreeders.com/bird/125434/blue-and-gold-macaw

Tel. No.: 239-898-6677

E-mail: Phloryda@gmail.com

Price: $1,800.00

Fancy Feathers

31 Roseland Avenue, Caldwell, New Jersey

Website: www.fancyfeathersaviary.com

Tel. No.: 973-403-2900

E-mail: ddargenio@gmail.com

Price: $1,650.00

Ara Aviaries California

Agoura Hills Los Angeles, California

Website: www.aracaris.com

Tel. No.: 805-338-3549

Email: billysaylors6@gmail.com

Price: $1,500.00

Pet Paradise

35535 Euclid Avenue, Willoughby, Ohio

Website: www.petparadiseohio.com

Tel. No.: 440-942-9016

E-mail:info@petparadiseohio.com

Price: $1,599.99

Delorce's Bird Barn

Charleston, South Carolina 29429

Website: www.delorcesbirdbarn.com

Tel. No.: 8432161553 or 8438198618

Email: brendabrinson1234@gmail.com

Price: $1,500.00

Green Parrot Superstore

8165 S. State Rd, Goodrich, Michigan

Website: www.greenparrotsuperstore.com

Tel. No.: 810-636-9120

greenparrotsuperstore@gmail.com

Price: $1,795.00

Merrick's Parrots

Morgan Hill, California 95037

Website: parrotparties.com

Tel. No.: 408-464-6125

E-mail: parrotsbyrenee@yahoo.com

Price: $1,800.00

Beaks and Feathers

1262 Airport Pulling Rd N, Naples, Forida 34104

Website: http://www.Facebook.com/BeaksandFeatherNaples

Tel. No.: 239-234-6092

E-mail: Beaksandfeathersinc@yahoo.com

Price: $2,200.00

Ana's Parrots

East Stroudsburg, PA 18301

Website: https://www.facebook.com/PoconoAna

Tel. No.: 646-496-5005

E-mail: poconoana@yahoo.com

Price: $1,800.00

Blue Throat or Caninde Macaw Breeders

The Bird Hut

Nashville, Tennessee 37221

Website: www.the-bird-hut.com

Tel. No.: 615-739-0631

E-mail: midtnecho@yahoo.com

Price: $1,999.00

River City Parrots

Mechanicsville, Virginia 23111

Website: http://www.birdbreeders.com/breeder/826/river-city-parrots-mechanicsville-VA

Tel. No.: 804-730-5540

E-mail:rivercityparrots@aol.com

Price: $4,000.00

Glamour Beaks

Loxahatchee, Forida 33470

Website:

http://www.birdbreeders.com/breeder/12114/glamour-beaks-loxahatchee-FL

Tel. No.: 561-350-1693

E-mail: glamourbeaks@gmail.com

Price: $1,700.00

Merrick's Parrots

Morgan Hill, California 95037

Website: www.parrotparties.com

Tel. No.: 408-464-6125

E-mail: parrotsbyrenee@yahoo.com

Price: $2,800.00

Delorce's Bird Barn

Charleston, South Carolina 29429

Website: www.delorcesbirdbarn.com

Tel. No.: 8432161553 or 8438198618

Email: brendabrinson1234@gmail.com

Price: $1,800.00

Green-Wing Macaw

Eggs-otic Parroting

Camino, California 95709

Website: www.eggsoticparroting.com

Tel. No.: 530-644-1846

Email: eggs-oticparroting@sbcglobal.net

Price: $2,100.00

Mountain Ridge Aviaries

Mount Solon, Virginia 22843

Website: www.mountainridgeaviary.com

Tel. No.: 540-886-2424

Email: bzybeaks@aol.com

Price: $2,100.00

Pets with Attitude

West Columbia, South Carolina 29170

Website: www.facebook.com/pages/Pets-with
Attitude/331470097012225
Tel. No.: 803-223-3255
Email: beaksattitude@aol.com
Price: $2,000.00

In A Pickle Parrots

7924 Broadview Road, Broadview Heights, Ohio 44147
Website: www.inapickleparrots.com
Tel. No.: 440-627-6477
Email: Inapickleaviary@aol.com
Price: $2,100.00

Brightwood Aviary

Dawsonville, Georgia 30534
Website: www.brightwoodaviary.com
Tel. No.: 770- 889-0353
Email: mom2mini@bellsouth.net
Price: $1,500.00

Lone Palm Aviary

Loxahatchee, Florida 33470
Website: www.lpbirds.com
Tel. No.: 570-730-1366
Email: jessica@lpbirds.com
Price: $500.00

Cindy's Parrot Place

Chesapeake, Virginia 23321

Website: http://www.cindysparrotplace.com

Tel. No.: 1-844-572-7768

Email: info@cindysparrotplace.com

Price: $2,500.00

World of Birds

15 Perry Street, Chester, New Jersey 07930

Website: www.worldofbirds.com

Tel. No.: 908-879-2291

Email: worldofbirds@optonline.net

Price: Negotiable

Birds By Joe LLC

1309 Bound Brook Road, Middlesex, NJ 08846

Website: www.birdsbyjoe.com

Tel. No.: 732-764-2473

Email: service@birdsbyjoe.com

Price: $2,300.00

Hahns Macaws Breeders

Beaker's Parrot Place

197 Wilkeson, Washington 98396

Website: www.BeakersParrotPlace.com

Tel. No.: 360-829-6643

Email: Info@beakersparrotplace.com

Price: Negotiable

Thea's Parrot Place

Fallbrook, California 92028

Website: www.theasparrotplace.com

Tel. No.: 760-842-3436

Email: theasparrotplace@att.net

Price: $1,250.00

Kedzie Parrot Place

East Lansing, Michigan 48823

Website: www.kedzieparrotplace.com

Tel. No.: 517-204-3878

Email: kedzieparrotplace@hotmail.com

Price: $925.00

Tail Feathers

Durand, Illinois 61024

Website: http://www.birdbreeders.com/breeder/38015/tail-feathers-durand-IL

Tel. No.: 815-248-4035

Email: tgsmall49@live.com

Price: $900.00

In A Pickle Parrots

7924 Broadview Road, Broadview Heights, Ohio 44147

Website: www.inapickleparrots.com

Tel. No.: 440-627-6477

Email: Inapickleaviary@aol.com

Price: $850.00

Hyacinth Macaws

Toucan Jungle

Vista, CA 92084

Website: www.ToucanJungle.com

Tel. No.: 760-672-0127

Email: Chris@Toucanjungle.com

Price: $1,300.00 - $10,000.00

Bird Farm

Homosassa, Florida 34446

Website: www.birdfarm.com/

Tel. No.: 352-503-6817

Email: birdfarmsales@onecom.com

Price: $ 11,599

C&C Farms Aviary

Windsor, Ontario

Website: www.ccaviary.com/

Tel. No.: 519-726-6698

Email: ccfarms@bell.net

Price: $20,000

BirdsNow.com

Website: http://www.birdsnow.com/hyacinthmacaw.htm

Price Ranges: $600 - $4,000

Blue-Winged or Illigers Macaws

All Birds Feathered Treasures

St. Charles, MO 63304

Website: www.knrfeatheredtreasures.com

Tel. No.: 636-928-5196

Email: kfeatheredtreasures@gmail.com

Price: $1,300.00

The Bird Hut

Nashville, Tennessee 37221

Website: www.the-bird-hut.com

Tel. No.: 615-739-0631

E-mail: midtnecho@yahoo.com

Price: $1,400.00

Lone Palm Aviary

Loxahatchee, Florida 33470

Website: www.lpbirds.com

Tel. No.: 570-730-1366

Email: jessica@lpbirds.com

Price: $1,800.00 (pair)

Birds By Joe LLC

1309 Bound Brook Road, Middlesex, NJ 08846

Website: www.birdsbyjoe.com

Tel. No.: 732-764-2473

Email: service@birdsbyjoe.com

Price: $1,599.00

Military Macaws

Avian Events, LLC

Conyers, GA 30094

Website: www. avianevents.com

Tel. No.: 770-500-2882

Email: tom@avianevents.com

Price: $1,000.00

Merrick's Parrots

Morgan Hill, California 95037

Website: www.parrotparties.com

Tel. No.: 408-464-6125

E-mail: parrotsbyrenee@yahoo.com

Price: $3,500.00 (pair)

Delorce's Bird Barn

Charleston, South Carolina 29429

Website: www.delorcesbirdbarn.com

Tel. No.: 8432161553 or 8438198618

Email: brendabrinson1234@gmail.com

Price: $1,500.00

Red-Front Macaws

The Bird Nerd

1818 Sanctuary Rd, Naples, Florida

Website: http://www.birdbreeders.com/bird/125434/blue-and-gold-macaw

Tel. No.: 239-898-6677

E-mail: Phloryda@gmail.com

Price: $ 2,200.00

AZ Parrots

Glendale, Arizona

Website: www.azparrots.com

Tel. No.: 623-266-3991

Email: dee@azparrots.com

Price: $1,495

Scarlet Macaws

Birds 4 Sale

Salem, OR 97306

Website: http://www.birdbreeders.com/bird/125336/scarlet-macaw

Tel. No.: 503-000-0000

Email: gr97024@gmail.com

Price: $895.00

Bevendale Farm & Aviary

Norwood Young America, MN 55368

Website: http://www.birdbreeders.com/bird/124268/scarlet-macaw

Tel. No.: 952-687-7357

Email: bevendalefza@gmail.com

Price: $1,100.00

Ginos Exiotic Birds

Blue Jay, CA 92317

Website: http://www.birdbreeders.com/bird/123210/scarlet-macaw

Tel. No.: 176-095-604-66

Email: Gmorrialle@gmail.com

Price: $4,000.00

Parrot Mutations
South West Florida 33982

Website: www.parrotmutations.com

Tel. No.: 941-623-3942

Email: lithol@aol.com

Price: $1,850.00

In A Pickle Parrots
7924 Broadview Road, Broadview Heights, Ohio 44147

Website: www.inapickleparrots.com

Tel. No.: 440-627-6477

Email: Inapickleaviary@aol.com

Price: $1,650.00

The Bird Hut
Nashville, Tennessee 37221

Website: www.the-bird-hut.com

Tel. No.: 615-739-0631

E-mail: midtnecho@yahoo.com

Price: $1,600.00

Merrick's Parrots
Morgan Hill, California 95037

Website: www.parrotparties.com

Tel. No.: 408-464-6125

E-mail: parrotsbyrenee@yahoo.com

Price: $3,750.00 (pair)

Ana's Parrots

East Stroudsburg, PA 18301

Website: https://www.facebook.com/PoconoAna

Tel. No.: 646-496-5005

E-mail: poconoana@yahoo.com

Price: $1,900.00

C&C Farms Aviary

Windsor, Ontario

Website: www.ccaviary.com/

Tel. No.: 519-726-6698

Email: ccfarms@bell.net

Price: $3,500

Severe Macaws

JC Aviary

Austin, TX 78748

Website: www.jcaviary.com

Tel. No.: 512-956-0937

Email: 512-956-0937

Price: $1,150.00

In A Pickle Parrots

7924 Broadview Road, Broadview Heights, Ohio 44147

Website: www.inapickleparrots.com

Tel. No.: 440-627-6477

Email: Inapickleaviary@aol.com

Price: $1,150.00

Cindy's Parrot Place

Chesapeake, Virginia 23321

Website: http://www.cindysparrotplace.com

Tel. No.: 1-844-572-7768

Email: info@cindysparrotplace.com

Price: $1,850.00

Gold/Yellow-Collared Macaws

Bird Farm

Homosassa, Florida 34446

Website: www.birdfarm.com

Tel. No.: 352-503-6817

Email: birdfarmsales@onecom.com

Price: $ 899

BirdsNow.com

<http://www.birdsnow.com/yellowcollared.htm>

Price Ranges: $800 - $1,000

Buffon's Macaw

C&C Farms Aviary

Windsor, Ontario

Website: www.ccaviary.com/

Tel. No.: 519-726-6698

Email: ccfarms@bell.net

Price: $7,500

Boxess

Southern Oregon

Website:www.boxess.com/buffons.htm

Email: boxess@boxess.com

Price: Not listed

Blue-Headed Macaws

Lone Palm Birds

Website: www.lpbirds.com

Tel. No.: 570-730-1366

Email: jessica@lpbirds.com

Price: $6500.00

c.) Local Macaw Breeders in Great Britain

Here are the website links and contact details of local Macaw breeders in Great Britain:

Blue-and-Gold Macaws

DJR Hobbybreeders

Folkestone, Kent

Tel. No.: 01303252556

Link: <http://www.pets4homes.co.uk/classifieds/1301383-baby-handreared-blue-gold-macaw-folkestone.html>

Price: £1,499

Private Advertiser

Ebbw Vale, Blaenau Gwent

Tel. No.: 01495308893

Link: <http://www.pets4homes.co.uk/classifieds/1293522-blue-and-gold-macaw-with-large-cage-ebbw-vale.html>

Price: £900

Private Advertiser

Reading, Berkshire

Tel. No.: 07831539705

Link: <http://www.pets4homes.co.uk/classifieds/1303569-young-blue-gold-macaw-need-new-home-reading.html>

Price: £1,200

Private Advertiser

Sheffield, South Yorkshire

Tel. No.: 097748188285

Link: http://www.pets4homes.co.uk/classifieds/1298801-blue-and-gold-macaw-talking-parrot-mega-tame-sheffield.html

Price: £2,000

Private Advertiser

Birmingham, West Midlands

Tel. No.: 07493274356

Link: <http://www.pets4homes.co.uk/classifieds/1292442-semi-tame-blue-and-gold-macaw-with-cage-birmingham.html>

Price: £795

Private Advertiser

Smethwick, West Midlands

Tel. No.: 07914151120

Link: <http://www.pets4homes.co.uk/classifieds/1261169-blue-and-yellow-macow-smethwick.html>

Price: £1,200

Scarlet Macaws

Private Advertiser

Salford, Greater Manchester

Tel. No.: 07590262996

Link: <http://www.pets4homes.co.uk/classifieds/1310594-scarlet-macaw-salford.html>

Price: £2,000

Private Advertiser

Enfield, Middlesex

Tel. No.: 07539227023

Link: <http://www.pets4homes.co.uk/classifieds/1298855-scarlet-macaw-ara-macao-enfield.html>

Price: £1,500

Hanhs Macaws

Private Advertiser

Fordingbridge, Hampshire

Tel. No.: 07967942213

Link: <http://www.pets4homes.co.uk/classifieds/1303365-bonded-pair-hahns-mccaws-fordingbridge.html>

Price: £650

Private Advertiser

Liverpool, Merseyside

Tel. No.: 07961146837

Link: <http://www.pets4homes.co.uk/classifieds/1285723-hahns-macaw-parrot-liverpool.html>

Price: £400

Green-Winged Macaw

Private Advertiser

Uxbridge, Middlesex

Tel. No.: 07736544431

Link: <http://www.pets4homes.co.uk/classifieds/1300442-green-winged-macaw-uxbridge.html>

Price: £950

UK Breeder Websites

Barrett Watson Parrots

< http://www.barrettwatsonparrots.co.uk/?p=macaws>

Hand Reared Parrots

<http://www.handrearedparrots.co.uk/>

Remarks: Blue-and-gold macaw; Green-winged macaw only

Bird Trader

<http://www.birdtrader.co.uk/>

PreLoved

<http://www.preloved.co.uk/search?keyword=Macaws>

Selecting a Healthy Macaw

Macaws on average can live for up to 60 years and more! These birds are long time companions, and its longevity highly depends on how your chosen breeders took care of them especially when they were young.

This section will give you simple tips on how you can spot a healthy macaw that you can keep for life!

a.) Signs of a Healthy Macaw Bird

Look out for these signs so that you know if your prospect bird is healthy:

- The bird should be active, alert, and sociable
- It should eat and drink throughout the day
- It should have dry nostrils and bright, dry eyes
- The beak, legs, and feet should have normal appearance
- It should have a dry and clean vent
- Its feathers should be smooth and well-groomed

Chapter Five: Maintenance for Macaws

Assuming that you have already bought a Macaw as your pet, the responsibility that comes with it is the most crucial part of the process. You as the owner, have to provide for its basic needs so that it will be healthy and happy. In this chapter you will learn the different requirements needed for your bird such as its cage, accessories and food necessary for the maintenance of your Macaw.

Habitat and Environment

Macaws have adapted well to human-modified habitats, such as parks and gardens in villages and towns. Like other kinds of birds, Macaws should be kept in a bird-safe environment. As the owner you need to have knowledge of its habitat requirements and environmental conditions to ensure that your bird is healthy. You will find tons of information in this section regarding the maintenance your pet needs in order to keep them happy.

a.) Ideal Cage Size for Macaws

There are lots of macaw species and each type differs in size, which makes it impossible to recommend only one cage size that could fit them all, however a general guideline that you can follow when it comes to bird cages is that, the parrot should be able to move around and flap its wings without touching the sides of the cage.

As for macaws, it is also advisable to buy a durable cage preferably with locks to prevent them from escaping because they are naturally curious and quite mischievous.

For mini-macaws or smaller types of macaws, you can buy a 34x 24 x 36 cage with at least ¾ inch to 1 inch bar spacing; for large macaws a 36 x 48 x 60 cage size is all you need with at least 1 to 2 inches bar spacing. When it comes to buying cages, bigger is always better!

It is also advisable that the cage material uses non-toxic paint or else it can cause your pet to be poisoned by metal. It shouldn't also be made out of brass either because it contains zinc which could kill your parrot as well.

Ideally the cage should also have at least three doors. One as the main entrance and the other two should be used for food and water.

Your bird will be spending most of their lives inside the cage that's why it needs to be large so that it can also accommodate lots of toys and perches.

b.) Cage Maintenance

Your parrot's cage could affect the health of your pet so it's very important that you check it daily for any dirt, like its feces and spoiled food left in perches and cups to prevent health problems.

You should also change the cage paper every other day as well as check the metal parts & bars of your bird's cage periodically for chipped paint and rust, because your bird will most likely chew or swallow the flaked pieces.

You should be able to clean the cage thoroughly at least once every month. You could use a mild dishwashing liquid or bleach with warm water for about a minute. Then rinse all soap and bleach thoroughly with water before letting your bird inside the cage.

c.) Location of the Cage

Finding the perfect cage is just as important as knowing where to place it. As established earlier, macaws are noisy and loud creatures that's why you should take that into consideration when finding a good location for your bird.

Put them in a place where they'll get to interact with people, and won't be too much of a disturbance at the same time – if in case they screech and scream.

Put the cage at an eye level to create a sense of confidence in your bird and place the cage in a higher location so that they would feel secure just like in the wild.

Avoid placing the cage in a window because the sun can cause your parrot to become ill due to too much heat. Find the right balance between the sunlight and an appropriate amount of shade for your macaw.

Finding the right location of the cage could lessen stressful situations for your bird so that they can enjoy their life with their new owner.

d.) Recommended Supplies

Now that your cage is all set and you already have an idea on where to properly place it, you need to provide supplies to meet its needs. Here are the recommended supplies that your Macaws needs:

Perches

The main purpose of perches is to exercise your bird's feet; it could also prevent sores and foot related health issues in the future. In the wild, birds especially Macaws, are used to transferring from one tree to another but in captivity of course they can't do that, so a great alternative is to buy them perches, preferably made out of fresh fruit tree branches. The minimum area for the perch is about ¾ in diameter.

You'll need different types of perches such as wood dowel, natural branch type, a therapeutic perch or a cement perch as well as Eucalyptus branches, just make sure that it is not poisonous. Macaws love to chew them and because of that you may have to replace it regularly. There are lots of perches you could choose from especially from online stores. These perches could also be used as ropes and swings for your pet. Do not also put the perch above the bird's bowl or dishes otherwise the food and water will be contaminated.

Toys

Macaws are very fond of chewing, you may find yourself regularly buying and replacing new toys to keep them happy. It is recommended that you purchase toys that are easy to be destroyed, it'll be very interactive for your macaw to prevent boredom. However, if you're in a tight budget, you can also buy toys that are durable so that it could last longer. Toys specifically designed for Macaws are quite expensive than regular ones. It is not advisable to put all of the toys inside your bird's cage because it will become dirty and overcrowded. Rotate the toys at least once a week.

Dishes

Buy at least 3 sturdy dishes; one for fresh water, one for pellet or seed mix and one for fresh foods. Avoid buying plastic dishes because your Macaw will most likely break it and it could also be harmful on its health. Place it away from the perches so that it would not be contaminated with bird droppings.

Formulated Diet

Some Macaw owners feed their birds only with seeds, while some only provides a pellet diet; this however could limit the nutrients your pet is receiving. Experts suggest that parrots should be given a variety of food for a balanced nutrition or what they call a formulated diet.

Macaws are very energetic parrots that's why a good combination of formulated diet: fruits and vegetables as well as a good amount of protein and other nutrients plus clean water is essential to keep their bodies healthy and active. You will need a good supply of packaged pellet diet, to be mixed with seed. Then you can slowly add fresh foods and protein. Formulated bird food may already contain vitamins so it's not recommended that you give another one separately unless prescribed by your vet. Conversion takes about a week or so depending on your bird and how well you feed them.

Treats

Macaws, like other parrots can be taught to perform tricks, but of course, it always comes with a price! You can give your pet different types of treats such as fruits, seed and spray as well as Do-It-Yourself (DIY) treats like pretzels, popcorn or something healthy that your bird can munch on. Later in this book, you will be provided with a list of recommended treats as well as treats you should avoid.

e.) Bird Bath for Macaws

Macaws needs a regular bath to maintain a good skin condition, here are some things you need to know on how to maintain your bird's hygiene and keep a healthy life.

Provide a misting bottle or a birdbath. All birds should be gently misted with a water bottle at room temperature. The spray should be sprayed up over the bird much like a shower rain, never spray the bird directly in its face.

It's important that you keep an eye in your bird while it is bathing. Bathe your Macaw with clean water. Distilled water is sometimes required. Speak to your veterinarian on the best choice of water for your bird. During its misting and bathing procedures, make sure there are no drafts because it can cause respiratory issues. It may chill your bird when he is wet. Use towels and blankets, but be careful because it can catch the bird's nails and beaks in their threads.

To ensure that the oils from their skin glands, disease organisms or items such as lotions and hand creams do not transfer to your bird's feathers, wash your hands with soap and water thoroughly before handling your Macaw.

Your bird may be ill if it seems to stop grooming and becomes dirty. Once you see this signs, contact your avian veterinarian immediately.

f.) Lighting and Temperature

The average room temperature for your bird should not exceed 80 degrees. Avoid drafty areas that will get direct heat from sun for any portion of the day.

Parrots also have tetra-chromic vision (4 color light vision including ultraviolet), that's why a full color light bulb must be present in the cage area. The incandescent or monochromatic light bulbs usually found in households are not a good choice for your Macaw.

Cover the cage during nighttime or at least provide a shade to block out any excess light and also creates a more secure sleeping place. Be careful when using fabrics as cover because your bird might rip it with its claws or beak and could likely eat it.

Never ever place the cage in the kitchen or somewhere near cooking fumes because bird's can be very sensitive, that even a small amount of smoke can be fatal.

Diet and Feeding

In the wild, Macaws primarily eat palm nuts, seeds and fruits. Since these birds are very active, they will need nutrients that are rich in calories, protein and oil among others.

Fortunately, today's supplements have opened new and healthy options for pet owners. In this section you will be guided on how to properly feed your parrot and learn the feeding amount and nutritional requirements they need.

a.) Nutritional Needs of Macaws

Feeding your Macaw is not that complicated. However, its level of activity should be taken into consideration to meet its nutritional diet. They're not choosy eaters but like what was mentioned earlier, it is highly recommended that parrots should be given a variety of food for a balanced nutrition.

As much as possible avoid only giving the same type of food such as a pellet diet or seed diet only; it can result in nutrient deficiency and may lead to diseases due to its limited nutrients, which could also shorten the life expectancy of your parrot.

This section outlines the foods your pet will appreciate in order to meet the majority of its dietary needs.

b.) Types of Food

Seeds and Pellet

Seeds are a big part of any bird's diet; they eat seeds naturally in the wild and it is also a good source of Carbohydrates. However, seeds alone can cause complications because it is naturally fatty. Although macaws need fatty acids for their skin development, it still should be moderated. It is not advisable that you mixed seeds with pellets and feed it off right away, although a lot of people do recommend that; for best results offer seeds first for a few days, then slowly incorporate pellets into the diet until your Macaw gets well adjusted.

The key is to give it in moderation. Feed them at least 1/2 - 3/4 cup of fortified parrot mix or diet, the amount may be vary depending on the size of your macaw.

Fresh Vegetables

Vegetables contain Phytonutrients that enhance the body's immune system which prevents illnesses. Veggies are also a rich source of natural fiber for the body. However, keep in mind that you should feed them with vegetables in moderation to prevent diarrhea and make sure they are properly washed before feeding it to your bird.

Below is the list of highly recommended vegetables for Macaws:

- Artichoke
- Asparagus
- Beets and greens
- Broccoli and greens
- Cabbage
- Carrots
- Cauliflower and greens

- Celery
- Chard
- Chickweed
- Chicory
- Chinese Cabbage
- Cucumber
- Dandelion Greens
- Edamame
- Eggplant
- Fennel and leaves, stems, seeds
- Kale
- Leeks
- Lettuce (darker is better)
- Mustard Greens
- Okra
- Peas/Snap Peas/String Beans/Snow Peas
- Peppers (all types)
- Radicchio
- Radish and greens
- Spinach
- Sweet Potato/Yam (cooked/parboiled)
- Squash (all types)
- Tomatoes (offer in moderation)
- Turnips and turnip greens
- Watercress
- Wheat Grass

- Yams

Fruits

Fruits are healthy and sweet; they also provide natural sources of sugars for the parrots. It is recommended that you only offer bite-sized fruits and do remove the pits or seeds of the fruits to prevent your macaw from choking.

Below are list of fruits that are highly recommended by veterinarians for your macaw:

- Apples (no seed)
- Apricots (no seed)
- Banana
- Blackberries
- Blueberries
- Cherries (no seed)
- Coconut (feed sparingly due to fat content)
- Cranberries
- Custard Apple
- Dragon Fruit
- Figs
- Guava
- Grapefruit
- Grapes
- Kiwi Fruit
- Lemon

- Lime
- Longan
- Lychee
- Mango (no seed)
- Melon (cantaloupe, watermelon, honeydew)
- Nectarine (no seed)
- Olive (fresh)
- Oranges
- Papaya
- Passion Fruit
- Peach (no seed)
- Pear (no seed)
- Pineapple
- Plum (no seed)
- Pomegranate
- Pomelo
- Quince
- Raspberries
- Rose Hips
- Rowan Berries
- Schizandra Berries
- Starfruit
- Strawberries
- Tamarillo
- Tangerine

Important Reminder:

Offer fruits and vegetables daily or every 2-3 days. As a caution, if your macaw didn't consume all the fruits you gave, remove all of its traces from the cage to avoid the risk of eating a spoiled fruit.

Vitamins

As mentioned earlier, some fortified parrot diet or parrot mix already contains essential vitamins. Before buying a good pellet mix or picking vegetables for your macaw, you should keep in mind that Vitamin A is one of the most essential vitamin birds need.

Vitamin A improves vision and can also boost immunity. Eggs and meat are good sources of Vitamin A as well as different types of vegetables like carrots, kale broccoli, sweet potatoes, cantaloupe and squash. Too much or not enough of Vitamin A can potentially leave your macaw vulnerable to diseases. Since macaws differ in types and sizes, it is best to consult with your avian veterinarian first to know the right amount of Vitamin A your pet needs.

Amino Acids

Macaws need high levels of protein or amino acids to build their tissues, feathers, muscles and skin. Birds in general can produce its own amino acids, however, there are some amino acids such as threonine, tryptophan, leucine, lysine, methionine, phenylalanine and valine that Macaws are unable to produce or sustain in its body. Fortunately, the sources of these essential amino acids are available in today's bird diet products.

Here is the list of recommended protein for your pet Macaws to feed on:

- Beans (cook small amounts as needed)
- Chicken (cooked, preferably shredded not fried)
- Eggs (cooked/hard boiled)
- Nuts (all types)
- Peanuts
- Seeds (birdseeds provide protein)
- Sprouts
- Turkey (cooked, preferably shredded)

Calcium

Calcium's primary role is to make bones grow stronger and it also allows calcification of eggshells in birds. Usually in the wild, macaws get their calcium and other minerals through clay deposits. In captivity, you can provide calcium in the form of a cuttlebone or calcium treat that is attached inside your bird cage. You can also offer a powdered supplement such as packaged oyster shell which can be added directly to your pet's food. Follow the instructions on the supplement package. Calcium is also vital for muscle contraction, blood clotting and heart functions.

Your macaw should be exposed to UVB light for at least 3-4 hours a day, for optimal physiologic use of the calcium you are giving to your bird.

Water

Hydration is just as important for birds as it is for human beings especially during hot weather conditions to avoid dehydration; macaws may drink 10 times its normal water intake during summer. They should be given access to clean, fresh and cool water. Do not use tap water because can cause the bird to be ill, as well as distilled water, instead use unflavored bottled drinking water or bottled natural spring water. If in case, tap water is used, treat it with a de-chlorinating treatment. Inability to provide fresh water to pet birds can cause upset stomach with unbearable stomachache.

Water is vital to maintain cells, digestion, feathers, and metabolism.

All water given to birds for drinking, as well as water used for misting, soaking or bathing must be 100% free of chlorine and heavy metals.

Treats

As mentioned earlier, you could give your parrots a reward every time they do something right like performing tricks or simply learning how to speak. You can feed them with different types of nuts such as almonds, macadamias, and walnuts. You can also give easy to digest and bite-sized fruits or Do-It-Yourself treats every now and then.

Some examples of DIY treats are carrot muffins (minus the sugar), popcorn, corn, unsalted pretzel sticks with fruits and brown rice with berries. They will surely love something appetizing to eat and this is also a positive reinforcement for the bird especially during training them.

c.) Toxic Foods to Avoid

Some foods are specifically toxic for your Macaws or any type of birds in general. Make sure that your bird never gets to eat one of the toxic items below and ensure that an avian veterinary checks your bird every now and then. These harmful foods is as important as selecting the right supplements and food items for your bird.

The following list of foods is highly toxic for your Macaw:

- Onions
- Alcohol
- Mushrooms
- Tomato Leaves

- Caffeine
- Dried Beans
- Parsley
- Chocolate (highly allergic)
- Avocados
- Junk Food
- Apple and Cherry Seeds
- Lettuce
- Milk and Dairy Products
- French fries,
- Marbled meat
- Peanut Butter
- Butter

Handling and Training Macaws

There would be instances that your pet will be out of its cage, especially for Macaws. These birds are very active and are natural explorers. However, it's also important to keep in mind on how to properly handle and train your Macaw so that it will not cause harm to itself and to people as well.

In this section, you'll learn some guidelines on how to confidently handle your parrot as well as some tips on trimming its nails, wings and beaks to maximize its balance, abilities and flying potential.

a.) Tips for Taming Your Macaw

Taming your macaw is the first thing to do before teaching them some cool tricks.

The flipside of owning a macaw is that they have quite a reputation for having a witty attitude and loves to scream a lot, in some cases they even tend to bite when feel threatened. The key is to figure out the level of your bird's comfort zone and remove it so that you could have a great bonding experience together. Here are some tips on how to do tame your macaw:

- Start by slowly touching your parrot in its beak. Carefully move your hand closer and closer towards its beak. If the parrot reacts or moves away, stop for a while.
- Wait for it to calm down, then take your hand away and give a treat.
- Practices repeating this procedure until you are able to fully touch its beak. Your macaw will eventually tolerate you in touching its beak and once you do, you can also scratch their beak. Just be extra careful when doing it, their beaks are sharp and really strong, but you have to conquer your fear if you want to get along with them!

b.) Tips for Training Your Macaw

Now that you and your macaw quite get along already, strengthen your relationship by training them. Training a macaw is not that hard to do, in fact it can be a fun and rewarding bonding experience for you and your feathered friend! There are lots of pet owners out there who have properly trained and raised a well-behaved macaw. They are clever creatures by nature, that is why they can absorb information very quickly and easily as long as you do it right.

Trust is the most important key in training your parrot. The first thing you need to do is to be able to establish a solid connection and rapport between you and your pet.

This section will provide some guidelines you can follow in getting your bird well behaved and disciplined. Are you ready? Read on!

Stepping Up is a basic skill your parrot should learn, to find out how to do this follow the tips below:

- A good way to pacify your bird into your hands without being forceful is to try and make your parakeet step up onto a handheld perch.
- Slowly and progressively begin training it to step up on your hand. If you are afraid of being bitten then wear gloves, but you may want to get rid of it

eventually because it might still encourage them to bite you because they can chew the leather.

- Hold your hand in a short distance away from your parrot so that when it tries to step into the target stick, it will have no choice but to step into your hand.

- Keep practicing until your parrot won't need your stick anymore. It will get accustomed and comfortable whenever you command it to step up in your finger

Grooming Your Macaw

a.) Trimming Your Macaw's Nails

Like many parrots, macaws have a very sharp, needle-like nails because they do a lot of climbing in the wild, and they also use these nails to dig into wood to keep them secure.

Unclipped nails can dig into the skin, leaving scratches or painful wounds to a person, only clipped to a point that the bird can perch securely and does not bother you when the bird is perched on your hand. Many people have their macaw's nails clipped to the point that it becomes dull and the bird can no longer grip a perch firmly. This can result to becoming more clumsy and nervous because it cannot move without slipping. This nervousness can develop into fear biting and panic attacks.

Another tip is only use a styptic powder on your bird's nails, not the skin!

b.) Trimming Your Macaw's Beaks

Macaws are known to have a strong and sharp beak; that is what makes them different from other types of birds. They are very fond of chewing and pecking everything they can get into. However, if not properly or regularly trimmed, beaks may result into deformity.

Consult a qualified veterinarian to show you the proper way in trimming your pet's beaks. You can also check out several grooming items such as lava and mineral blocks that are available in your local pet store, to keep their beaks in great shape.

c.) Clipping a Macaw's Wings

Birds are design to fly, young macaws can be fairly clumsy and flying gives them confidence as well as agility, stamina, and muscle tone.

Before clipping their wings, make sure that your macaws are flying, maneuvering and landing well already. If they do not learn how to properly land by lifting their wings and flaring their tail, then when they are clipped, they could injure themselves and could also break their beak or keel bone.

Consult a qualified veterinarian to show you the proper way in clipping a bird's wings. A certain amount of flight feathers will be removed while leaving the smaller balancing feathers inside the wing closer to the body uncut.

Chapter Six: Breeding Macaws

If you decided to buy two macaws, for instance a male and female and keep them together, you should definitely prepare for the possibility of breeding, unless it's the same gender, otherwise you're going to be caught off guard!

If you are interested in breeding your macaw, this chapter will give you a wealth of information about the processes and phases of its breeding and you will also learn how to properly breed them on your own. This is not for everyone but if you want to have better understanding about how these birds procreate, then you should definitely not miss this part! On the contrary if you are interested in becoming a reputable breeder, then this is a must read chapter for you.

Basic Macaw Breeding Info

Before deciding if you truly want to become a breeder, you should at least have prior knowledge on their basic reproduction process and breeding. This section will inform you on how these creatures procreate.

a.) Sexual Dimorphism

Macaws are not sexually dimorphic; males and females are visually identical in both min-macaws and large macaws. You can only determine it through DNA analysis, which uses sample blood or feathers. Although, some breeders claim that they can distinguish if the bird is male or female because of its features, it is still indefinite unless it's DNA is tested.

DNA Sexing or Surgical Sexing can also provide additional information on its sexual maturity and capability to reproduce. It is inexpensive and convenient so if you like to know more about your bird's sexuality you should definitely give it a try. Some veterinarians might also try chromosomal analysis on your macaw to determine its gender.

b.) Mating and Reproduction

Mini-macaws such as Yellow-collared, Hahn's, and Illiger's reaches sexual maturity at around 4 – 6 years, while large macaws such as Blue & Gold macaws, Scarlet, Military, Hyacinth and Green-winged macaws are sexually matured at 5 – 7 years old but it does not necessarily mean that the parrots are suitable to start breeding.

Large and mini-macaws are typically monogamous when it comes to finding its mate. The breeding period for these birds usually occurs year-round but mostly it happens during spring or early summer.

Generally, on average females lay about 2 – 4 eggs per clutch and incubation starts after the first egg is laid, it usually takes about 26 - 28 days. The chicks become independent and leave the nest in usually 2 – 3 months.

It is highly recommended that you provide an additional 20% increase on fatty seeds as well as their intake of vitamin supplements and proteins such as hard-boiled egg and shredded chicken during the breeding process.

It's also important to note that the incubation temperature should be kept between 37.2° - 37.3 °C (99.1°- 99.2°F) and the wet bulb temperature should at least be 26° - 28°C or (80°- 82° F) before the eggs are hatched.

The Macaw Breeding Process

In order to have a clear sketch of how Macaws reproduce, this section will show you the breeding process and the information you need to know, so that your pets can successfully procreate.

a.) Selecting Macaws for Breeding

For you to select a healthy, fertile and active parrot it is recommended that your parrot undergoes clinical examination by a veterinarian. This is essential to determine if your parrot is capable of reproduction or not and at the same time it can prevent diseases that could be transmitted to the coming flock.

b.) Setting up a Good Nesting Environment

Macaws in the wild usually nest in tree hollows or cliff openings; in captivity, you need to set up a nice environment to replicate that natural breeding and dwelling place so that they can successfully mate and create healthy clutches. The nest box size should ideally measure 12 x12 x 36 inches with a minimum size of no less than 12 x 12 x 36 inches.

Keep in mind that the box should be three times the size of your macaw. It is highly recommended that the nest box is wide so that your macaws can have lots of space to move around and that it should ideally be made out of oak or wood.

The nest box typically has a circular or round entrance hole but since macaws are quite larger than the usual kinds of parrots, the hole should be square. Make sure that a strong wire is attached to the outside walls of the nest to prevent from escaping and do not hang it on the wall like other parrots' nests, macaws are strong and will chew on anything so to avoid breaking the nest box, put it on a platform instead.

c.) Nesting Materials

If you prefer to build your own nest box instead of buying one, you have to make sure that the materials you use are strong so that it will have a good foundation otherwise, your macaws could easily destroy it.

You should also put short pieces of wood or wood chips inside the box for your birds to chew; you can also give them bite-sized timber. This may help the breeders increase the percentage of fertile eggs and synchronize their breeding cycle as well.

d.) Brooding and Incubation

Breeding season happens usually around the months of February to June. Large macaws have one clutch per year while smaller macaws have 2 – 3 clutches. On average females lay about 2 – 4 eggs per clutch and incubation starts after the first egg is laid, it usually takes about 26 - 28 days. There is a 3 day interval for larger macaws while smaller macaws' interval after the first egg is 2 – 3 days. The chicks become independent and leave the nest in usually 2 – 3 months.

e.) Hatching

On average, the eggs hatch in about 24 - 48 hours after the incubation period for all types of macaws and it takes about 2 - 3 months before the young macaws leave the nest. Consult your vet on the suitable type of diet and vitamins or supplements needed for your baby macaws.

Hybridization of Macaws

Hybrid macaws are very common because of the wonderful mixture of colors they have and its interracial qualities. Plus, hybrids costs way more than regular macaws, so it's favorable for pet traders. Some examples of hybrid macaws are the Calico macaw, Shamrock macaw, Miligold macaw, Harlequin macaw, Camelot, and Catalina macaw.

There are three generations of hybrid macaws; the first-generation hybrid is a crossing of two natural occurring macaw species. The second-generation hybrid is a natural macaw specie combined with a first-generation hybrid, while the third-generation hybrid is the product of crossing hybrid macaws (either first or second generation). There are only a few third-generation hybrids of macaws.

Some bird enthusiasts and experts are against the practice of hybridization because it affects the naturally occurring macaw population. If you would like to breed a hybrid macaw, it is best to consult with your avian veterinarian first to check if your parrot has the capability to reproduce and to also avoid diseases.

a.) List of Hybrid Macaw Breeders in United States

Below are the lists of local hybrid macaw breeders in United States, please be reminded that these macaws are doesn't come cheap. The rarer the species is the more expensive it could be.

Fancy Feathers

(Hybrid of Green-winged and Catalina Macaw)

31 Roseland Avenue, Caldwell, New Jersey

Website: www.fancyfeathersaviary.com

Tel. No.: 973-403-2900

E-mail: ddargenio@gmail.com

Price: $2,300.00

Delorce's Bird Barn

(Harlequin macaw)

Charleston, South Carolina 29429

Website: www.delorcesbirdbarn.com

Tel. No.: 8432161553 or 8438198618

Email: brendabrinson1234@gmail.com

Price: $1,900.00

Green Parrot Superstore

(Ruby Macaw)

8165 S. State Rd, Goodrich, Michigan

Website: www.greenparrotsuperstore.com

Tel. No.: 810-636-9120

greenparrotsuperstore@gmail.com

Price: $2,195.00

Ana's Parrots

(Maui Sunset Macaw)

East Stroudsburg, PA 18301

Website: https://www.facebook.com/PoconoAna

Tel. No.: 646-496-5005

E-mail: poconoana@yahoo.com

Price: $3,000.00

Cindy's Parrot Place

(Hybrid of Harlequin Macaws and Ruby Macaw)

Chesapeake, Virginia 23321

Website: http://www.cindysparrotplace.com

Tel. No.: 1-844-572-7768

Email: info@cindysparrotplace.com

Price: $2,300.00

Birds By Joe LLC

(Ruby Macaw)

1309 Bound Brook Road, Middlesex, NJ 08846

Website: www.birdsbyjoe.com

Tel. No.: 732-764-2473

Email: service@birdsbyjoe.com

Price: $2,200.00

Avian Events, LLC

(Shamrock Macaw)

Conyers, GA 30094

Website: www. avianevents.com

Tel. No.: 770-500-2882

Email: tom@avianevents.com

Price: $2,400.00

Chapter Seven: Keeping Macaws Healthy

You as the owner should be aware of the potential threats and diseases that could harm the wellness of your Macaws. Just like human beings, you need to have knowledge on these diseases so that you can prevent it from happening in the first place. You will find tons of information on the most common problems that may affect your bird including its causes, signs and symptoms, remedies and prevention.

Common Health Problems

In this section, you will learn about the diseases that may affect and threaten your macaw's wellness. Learning these diseases as well as its remedies is vital for you and your bird so that you could prevent it from happening or even help with its treatment in case they caught one.

Below are some of the most common health problems that occur specifically to Macaw parrots. You will learn some guidelines on how these diseases can be prevented and treated as well as its signs and symptoms.

Proventricular Dilation Disease

This disease is commonly known as Macaw Wasting Disease. It is an inflammatory wasting disease caused by a virus called Avian BornaVirus (ABV), which is mostly found in Psittacine species specially in Macaws. It primarily affects the Central Nervous System and multiple organs such as liver, kidneys, heart, brain, peripheral blood vessels, lungs and gastrointestinal tract.

a.) Cause and Effect

It is classified as a sporadic disease that has a very rare kind of attack to a bird's immune system. Unlike other virus which attacks the whole cell then move to another cell, ABV does not destroy the cells which leave the infected ones very little damage. Since the cells are not destroyed the immune system cannot detect it and thus the virus stays within the bird for an indefinite amount of time, which eventually weakens the immune system and results in continuous infections throughout the parrot's life.

c.) Diagnosis

Avian veterinarians have difficulties in detecting the virus because of other infections it can bring to the bird's health. The ABV does not show-up in the test results and there are other viruses similar to ABV which may also lead in the assumption that the bird is not a carrier even if it is.

d.) Signs and Symptoms

ABV is also an asymptomatic virus, which means that there are no signs that the bird might be infected or a carrier. However, sometimes you can notice it if your pet experienced instances of mild disorders such as moaning, feather-plucking or self-mutilation to severe illness such as head tremors, paralysis, seizures or other sudden sickness due to infected organs in the body.

e.) Treatment and Remedy

Veterinarians classified the severity of disease and level of impact to different stages such as low-to-moderate symptoms to severe and chronic stages.

Parrots in the early stages are given treatment to prevent the virus from spreading and eventually curing it. Although, this virus can be controlled and has a remedy, it's important that your bird always goes for checkup and undergo medical tests every now and then especially if it was diagnosed with the virus before.

Macaw Acne

Another common illness is the so called Macaw Acne. These are small swellings on the facial area of macaws particularly in the eyelids. It is caused by ingrown feathers on the face that causes irritation and infection.

a.) Treatment

Consult your veterinarian on the proper remedy to your macaw's acne, usually they would perform minor surgery to removed trapped feathers on the face or even suggest antibiotics such as cortico-steroids if the bird keeps scratching and rubbing the affected areas to prevent it from getting worse.

Coacal Papilloma

It is caused by a virus infection similar to warts in other animals and it is transmitted through direct contact. These tiny tumors usually appear in the vent area of a macaw where it can eventually block the fecal area of making it hard for the bird to defecate if it grows large enough.

a.) Treatment

The recommended treatment for this is a laser surgery. As a remedy veterinarians also advised owners to offer Jalapino peppers to prevent and control papilloma in birds. Consult your avian vet on the right amount of peppers to feed to your macaw.

Psittacosis or Parrot Fever

It is a zoonotic infectious disease caused by an unknown organism whose natural hosts are birds such as Macaws.

a.) Cause and Effect

It is an airborne disease and it can also be spread via the bird's feces. This disease is highly contagious. Before acquiring a Macaw, it's important that your bird goes through a Psittacosis test because this type of infection can also potentially harm a human being.

b.) Signs and Symptoms

The worst thing about this disease is that it is asymptomatic, which means symptoms does not appear or cannot be detected easily, you will never know when it could happen and if the bird is a carrier. Nevertheless, watch out for these possible signs that your pet might be having Psittacosis:

- Difficulty in breathing (due to Respiratory infections with airsac)
- Sneezing
- Runny eyes
- Congestion
- Liver disease might occur (and can progress rapidly to death)

c.) Diagnosis of Psittacosis

As mentioned earlier, this type of disease is asymptomatic that sometimes even a psittacosis test could not detect the disease. Identifying organisms in the feces is done in most cases.

d.) Treatment and Remedy

This disease is treated with a tetracycline based antibiotic given for about 45 days to eliminate the carrier state, although some veterinarians believe that the antibiotic does not necessarily remove the carrier state.

Pacheco's Disease

This disease is caused by a herpes virus which attacks the liver and results in acute liver failure. It is very contagious and highly fatal to most birds.

a.) Diagnosis

Diagnosis is done via necropsy which detects microscopic evidences of the virus found in the liver.

b.) Treatment and Remedy

Unfortunately, there is no guaranteed antibiotic or remedy for this disease, the best you could do is to minimize the spread of the virus through intensive care and some antiviral medication.

Aspergillosis

It is a respiratory disease caused by the fungus called *Aspergillus*, which is found in warm and moist environments.

a.) Cause and Effect

The microscopic spores of Aspergillus are an airborne transmitted disease. The fungus does not cause the disease per se but if your bird does not have a healthy immune system it can cause illness.

It increases the chances of the spores being inhaled by your bird if the environment has poor ventilation and sanitation, dusty conditions, and in close confinements.

Other predisposing factors include poor nutrition, other medical conditions in the respiratory system and prolonged use of antibiotics or corticosteroids, which eventually weakens the immune system. Aspergillosis is more common in parrots than other pet birds.

b.) Signs and Symptoms

There are two kinds of Aspergillosis, it's either acute or chronic, both of which attacks the respiratory system.

Acute Aspergillosis signs and symptoms include:

- Severe difficulty in breathing
- Cyanosis (a bluish coloration of mucous membranes and/or skin)
- Decreased or loss of appetite
- Frequent drinking and urination

Chronic Aspergillosis symptoms include:

- White nodules appear through the respiratory tissue
- Large numbers of spores enter the bloodstream
- Infection in the kidneys, skin, muscle,

gastrointestinal tract, liver, eyes, and brain

Other signs of Aspergillosis may include:

- Rapid breathing
- Exercise intolerance
- Change in syrinx (voice box); reluctance to talk
- Discharged and clogging of Nares
- Tremors
- Seizures or paralysis
- Green discoloration in the urates may be seen
- Enlarged liver
- Gout (painful, inflamed joints due to urate deposits)
- Depression and lethargy

c.) Diagnosis of Aspergillosis

Aspergillosis is generally difficult to detect until complete diagnosis. Do not compromise respiratory infections, consult the veterinarian immediately.

Here are some of the tests that your macaws needs to undergo through for diagnosis

- Radiographs (a complete blood count)
- Endoscopy (used to view lesions in the syrinx or trachea)
- PCR testing for the presence of Aspergillus

d.) Treatment and Remedy

Always consult a veterinarian first to know the right remedy for your bird. Another antifungal drug called Amphotericin B may be administered orally, topically, by injection, or nebulizing. Consult your vet for proper guidance. Surgery may also be performed to remove accessible lesions. Supportive care is often needed such as oxygen, supplemental heat, tube feeding, and treatment of underlying conditions.

e.) Prevention

Maintaining a good husbandry and diet can highly prevent outbreaks of Aspergillosis.

Below are some tips you can do to ensure that your bird is free from such a deadly disease:

- Keep your bird in a well-ventilated environment.
- Always clean the food and water dishes
- Thoroughly clean cages, toys, perches and other accessories at least once a month.
- Replace substrate (material lining the cage bottom) regularly
- Offer a good nutrition, such as the right combination of fruits, vegetables and seeds

Psittacine Beak and Feather Disease (PBFD)

PBFD is a viral condition that is responsible for damage to the beak, feathers and nails as well as the immune system of infected birds. These are very common in macaw species.

a.) Signs and symptoms

PBFD typically affects the feathers of infected birds as well as its beak and nails over time. Here are some signs and symptoms that your pet might have PBFD.

- Feathers are short, fragile, malformed, and prone to bleeding and breaking. Birds may first lose their the white, fine powder produced by specialized feathers to help maintain feather health when this happens more abnormal feathers will eventually develop.
- Beak has become glossy rather than the more typical matte appearance
- Nails and beak becomes brittle and malformed
- Significant loss of feathers (as the follicles become damaged)
- Loss of appetite (especially in young macaws)
- Regurgitation or continuous vomiting

b.) Diagnosis

Veterinarians will likely perform a PCR test to confirm the diagnosis. This test uses advanced techniques to look for the virus' DNA.

Most of the time PCR only needs a blood sample, but your veterinarian may also need to take a swab from your bird's mouth and vent.

Other kinds of test may include:
- Complete blood count and a chemistry panel tests.
- DNA test for specifically for PBFD

c.) Treatment

The majority of clinically affected birds will die within a few months to a year because there are no antiviral drugs available to fight the virus. Your avian veterinarian can only help keep your bird comfortable because this condition is painful for the bird and it also allows secondary infections to take hold. Some birds may survive for a few months they will ultimately die from this disease.

d.) Prevention

The only thing breeders and pet owners can do to prevent this deadly virus is to take pro-active steps but since you can't help the birds mingle with other birds as they travel from wholesaler to retail pet distributors to your home the best solution is to have your bird examined by an avian veterinarian and allow diagnostic testing.

It is also wise to take your bird for a yearly exam to make sure it stays healthy. Yearly exams can catch small issues before they get worse.

Tracheal Mites

Tracheal Mites are quite common in birds because it can infiltrate the bird's entire respiratory tract and the severity of the infection can vary greatly. Birds with mild infections may not show any signs but severe infections may produce symptoms including trouble breathing, wheezing or clicking sounds, open-mouth breathing, and excessive salivation.

a.) Cause and Effect

This disease can be transmitted through close contact with an infected bird and through airborne particles. It can also be passed through contaminated food or drinking water.

b.) Diagnosis

It is quite difficult to diagnose if your macaw has tracheal mites, veterinarians often recommend performing a tracheal swab to check under a microscope for further evalutation.

c.) Signs and Symptoms

Common signs include sneezing, wheezing or difficulty in breathing. Continuous obbing of the tail while breathing is also a sign that your macaw may have a respiratory problem. Tracheal mites also overlap with a number of other infections that has the same symptoms, so you need to make sure you have an accurate diagnosis.

d.) Treatment and Remedy

Medications are available to treat the disease, though dosage can be tricky and many birds die from tracheal mites. It is best to consult your veterinarian first before getting any treatment options available for tracheal mites.

Feather Plucking

Feather plucking is very common in birds, often stress is the most common cause of this behavior. When your macaw becomes stressed due to many reasons such as poor hygiene, or an unhealthy diet, it may start plucking out its own feathers. Another potential cause for feather plucking is parasite infection. Some birds also experience feather loss as the result of an iodine deficiency, though this is more common in finches than in macaws. If the feather loss is limited to the head, it is most likely due to aggression by other birds or a mite infection.

Other common types of disorders in macaws include:

- Mutilation
- Aggression
- Drug sensitivities
- Beak and Toe deformities in young macaws
- Respiratory infections
- Malcolored feathers
- Bacterial and viral infections
- Sunken eye sinusitis
- Allergies
- Reproductive disorders
- Feather cysts Syndrome

Recommended Tests

Here are the recommended tests your macaws should take and undergo to detect potential diseases and further evaluate its health condition so that it can be prevented and treated as soon as possible.

For young macaws, you might want to do a CBC or **Complete Blood Count**; this is a general test for birds and even humans to test for any internal infections. Another test is called **Chlamydophila Immunoassay**; this is a diagnosis exam to check if your bird might be carrying a contagious parrot fever, which is also potentially harmful to humans.

You might also want to do a **Culture diagnosis** to detect if there are any bacterial infections in your young macaws.

For adult macaws, a CBC and Culture diagnosis should be done regularly as prescribed by your avian veterinarian as well as a full body X-ray usually with gas sedation for further evaluation of your pet's condition. If there are any signs of illness, veterinarians will recommend further tests to identify your bird's potential disease.

Signs of Possible Illnesses

For you to keep your macaws healthy, you need to monitor them to ensure that they are in good condition, however there will come a time that your bird will get sick. Here are some early warning signs that your macaw could be potentially ill.

- **Activity** – Is your bird sleeping when it normally does not? Or being quiet when it normally isn't? Is there a decreased in food and water intake or not being able to eat at all like before?
- **Droppings** (feces) - Are there any change in urates (white part) or feces that is lasting more than 1-2 days?
- **Diarrhea** - Have you found undigested food in your bird's feces? Their droppings should have the three

distinct parts (green/brown, white and liquid urine). If you think your macaw has diarrhea, contact your vet immediately.

- **Weight loss** - Does your bird feels "light" when you pick it up? That maybe a sign of weight loss because the Keel bone becomes more prominent.
- **Feathers** – Is there a continuous presence of pinfeathers? It may be dull in color, broken, bent and fluffed up feathers.
- **Sneezing** – Is there a discharge in the nostrils when your bird sneezes? Look for stained feathers over the nares or crusty material in or around the nostrils.
- **Vomiting** – Has your pet been vomiting for quite a long period of time already? Macaws and all birds regurgitate occasionally as a sign of "affection" but it could also indicate a crop infection
- **Respiratory** – Are there signs of respiratory distress like tail bobbing up and down with each breath, a change in breathing sounds, and wheezing or clicking noise when it inhales?
- **Balance** – Has your bird been falling off its perch and huddling at the bottom of cage? It is a sign that it's losing its balance.
- **Eyes** – Does it appear dull? Is there a redness/swelling and loss of feathers around the eyes?
- **Feet** – Is it scaly or flaky? Does it have sores on the

bottom of the feet?

- **Head** – Have you noticed excessive head bobbing and shaking?
- **Beak** – Is your bird's beak swelling?
- **Behavior** – does your bird sits on the floor of its cage or habitat? Does it favor one foot over the other?

When these things happen, contact your avian veterinarian immediately. Do not compromise your bird's health; prevention is always better than cure.

Chapter Eight: Macaws Checklist

Congratulate yourself! You are now on your way to becoming a very well-informed and pro-active Macaw owner! Finishing this book is a huge milestone for you and your future or present pet bird, but before this ultimate guide comes to a conclusion, keep in mind the most important things you have acquired through reading this book.

This chapter will outline the summary of what you have learned, the do's and dont's as well as the checklist you need to tick off to ensure that you and your Macaw lived happily ever after!

Basic Information

- **Taxonomy**: phylum *Chordata*, class *Aves*, order *Psittaciformes*, family *Psittacidae*, Subfamily *Arinae*, Tribe *Arini*.
- **Distribution**: Mexico, Central and South America
- **Habitat**: Tropical Rainforests, Palm Swamp Forests
- **Lifestyle**: Flock Oriented
- **Anatomical Adaptations**:
- **Breeding Season**: February – June
- **Eggs**: 2 – 3 eggs per clutch
- **Incubation Period**: 26 - 28 days
- **Average Size**: 30cm - 100cm (11.8 to 39.5 in)
- **Average Weight**: 907grams - 1814 grams
- **Wingspan**: 86cm - 140cm (34in - 56in)
- **Top Speed**: 24km/h (15mph)
- **Coloration**: yellow, green, blue, white, red, orange, hybrid colors
- **Sexual Dimorphism**: Cannot be determine by physical characteristics; needs DNA testing
- **Conservation Status**: Endangered
- **Diet**: Seeds, Insects, Fruit, Nuts (Omnivore)
- **Sounds**: Vocal Communicator
- **Interaction**: Highly Social
- **Lifespan**: 50 - 60 years

Cage Set-up Guide

- **Minimum Cage Dimensions**: 34x 24 x 36 for mini-macaws; 36 x 48 x 60 for large macaws
- **Cage Shape**: the bigger, the better. Never purchase a round cage.
- **Bar Spacing**: ¾ inch to 1 inch bar spacing for mini-macaws; 1 to 2 inches bar spacing for large macaws.
- **Required Accessories**: food and water dishes, perches, grooming and cleaning materials, cuttlebone, toys
- **Food/Water Dish**: 3 sturdy dishes; one for fresh water, one for pellet/seed mix, and one for fresh foods. Do not buy dishes made out of plastic
- **Perches**: at least 3 different perches; wood dowel, natural branch type, a therapeutic perch or a cement perch or any fresh fruit tree branches
- **Recommended Toys**: rotate at least 3 different toys; rope toys, stainless steel bells, swings etc.
- **Bathing Materials**: misting bottle; bath tub
- **Nests Materials**: nest box made out of wood or oak
- **Recommended Temperature Range**: average temperature; it should not exceed 80 degrees.
- **Lighting:** full color light bulb must be present in the cage area. Do not use incandescent or monochromatic light bulbs.

Nutritional Information

- **Types of Recommended Food:**
- **Seeds:** 1/2 - 3/4 cup of fortified parrot seed mix
- **Fresh Fruits and Vegetables:** makes up about 15 to 20% of a Macaw's diet. Offer fruits and vegetables daily or every 2-3 days.
- **Supplements:** Calcium usually found in the form of a cuttlebone or Calcium treat. Powdered supplement such as packaged oyster shell can be added directly to your pet's food.
- **Amino Acids:** makes up about 20% of a Macaw's diet.
- **Carbohydrates:** makes up about 10% of a Macaws diet (nuts, seeds, corn etc.)
- **Water:** clean, fresh and cool water; unflavored bottled drinking water or bottled natural spring water

Breeding Information

- **Sexual Dimorphism**: They are not sexually dimorphic; gender can be identified through DNA sexing or chromosomal analysis.
- **Seasonal Changes**: breeding season usually begins in December or February and ends in June or July.
- **Sexual Maturity:** 4 – 6 years for mini-macaws; 5 – 7 years old for large macaws

- **Nest Box Size:** 12 x12 x 36 inches with a minimum size of no less than 12 x 12 x 36 inches during breeding period.
- **Egg Laying**: female lays eggs an average of 2 -3 eggs with an interval of 3 days.
- **Clutch Size**: one clutch per year for large macaws; 2 – 3 clutches for smaller or mini-macaws
- **Incubation Period**: 26-28 days
- **Hatching**: takes about 24 days to hatch
- **Chick Independence:** 2 – 3 months after hatching

Do's and Dont's

- Do keep them busy and happy;
- Do feed them a variety of nutritious food
- Do train them well to maximize their intelligence
- Do provide a clean and healthy environment
- Do give them time and commitment
- Do care for them when they feel ill
- Do provide plenty of toys inside the cage
- Do bond with them and let them out of the cage once in a while so that they can be exposed outside
- Do not use sandpaper covered perches or floor paper. It can cause severe damage to your bird's feet

- Do not use "bird disks" or "mite disks". These may harm your bird. See your avian veterinarian if you suspect parasites.
- Do not use bird gravel. Bird gravel is used for birds that do not crack the hull or shell of the seeds they eat. It causes severe impactions, which are often fatal. Gravel only benefits doves and pigeons definitely not parrots
- Do not use negative reinforcement during training because it is not effective
- Don't let macaws fall. It may contribute in developing respiratory problems and damages organs due to impact. Train them how to fly instead!
- Do not let your macaws get near to the following household items to prevent causes of accidents:
  - Ceiling or electric fans
  - Cooking oil
  - Leg chains
  - Toxic Fumes
  - Wood shavings
  - Toxic houseplants
  - Pesticides
  - Lead or zinc materials
  - Air fresheners
  - Scented candles
  - Sandpaper-covered perches
  - Tobacco and Cigarette smoke

Chapter Nine: Relevant Websites

Finishing this book doesn't mean that you should stop learning! This chapter provides you a wealth of references online that you could check out every now and then so that you can be updated when it comes to taking care of your Macaws. You can also find the websites you need to visit especially in buying cages and supplies for your pet.

Macaw Cage Links

Here is the recommended list of websites for you to choose from when buying cages both in United States and Great Britain.

United States Links:

For Large Macaws

Custom Cages
<https://www.customcages.com/catalogsearch/result/index/?q=Macaws&species=75>

Bird Cages 4 Less
<http://birdcages4less.com/page/B/CTGY/Macaw-Bird-Cages>

Bird Cages Now
<http://www.birdcagesnow.com/large-macaws/>

King's Cages
<http://www.kingscages.com/SearchResults.aspx?CategoryID=Cages&SubCatID=Large%20Macaw%20Cages%20Powder%20Coated>

Pet Solutions
<http://www.petsolutions.com/C/X-Large-Bird-Cages-Macaw-Large-Cockatoos.aspx>

<u>For Mini-Macaws</u>

Bird Cages 4 Less
<http://birdcages4less.com/page/B/CTGY/Mini-Macaw-Bird-Cages>

Bird Cages Now
<http://www.birdcagesnow.com/mini-macaws/>

Pets at Home
<http://www.petsathome.com/shop/en/pets/bird-and-wildlife/bird-cages>

Overstock
<http://www.overstock.com/Pet-Supplies/Bird-Cages-Houses/3643/cat.html>

Great Britain Links:

Cages World

<http://www.cagesworld.co.uk/f/Parrot_Cages/products::bird_type:Macaw.htm>

Northern Parrots (Small and Large Macaws)

<http://www.northernparrots.com/small-macaws-or-mini-macaws-deptb113/?>

<http://www.northernparrots.com/large-macaws-deptb112/?category=147>

Pebble – Home and Garden

<https://www.pebble.co.uk/compare.html?q=macaw%20cage>

Seapets

<https://www.seapets.co.uk/bird-supplies/bird-cages/macaw-cages>

Macaw Cage Accessories and Supplies

Here is the recommended list of websites for you to choose from when buying accessories such as toys, perches, dishes and other necessary supplies for your pet.

United States Links:

Doctors Foster and Smith – Toys
< http://www.drsfostersmith.com/bird-supplies/bird-toys/amazon-to-macaw-toys/ps/c/5059/5648/5704>

Fun Time Birdy - Toys
< http://www.funtimebirdy.com/patoyse.html>

Pet Mountain – Cleaning Supplies
< http://www.petmountain.com/category/311/1/bird-cage-cleaning-supplies.html>

PetSmart – Bowls, Feeders
<http://www.petsmart.com/bird/bowls-feeders/cat-36-catid-400014>

Wind City Parrot - Accessories
<http://www.windycityparrot.com/All_c_711.html>

Pet Solutions - Breeding Supplies

<http://www.petsolutions.com/C/Bird-Breeding-Supplies.aspx>

Bird Cages 4 Less - Perches

<http://birdcages4less.com/page/B/CTGY/Bird_Perches>

Pets at Home – Health Care Products

<http://www.petsathome.com/shop/en/pets/bird-and-wildlife/bird-healthcare-products>

Overstock - Accessories

<http://www.overstock.com/Pet-Supplies/Bird-Accessories/3646/cat.html>

Great Britain Links:

Cages World - Accessories
<http://www.cagesworld.co.uk/c/Bird_Cage_Accessories.htm>

Parrot Essentials - Accessories

<http://www.parrotessentials.co.uk/>

Parrotize UK – Parrot Stands and Covers

<http://parrotize.co.uk/products/parrot-stands/>

Seapets – Bird Toys

<https://www.seapets.co.uk/bird-supplies/bird-toys>

ZooPlus – Accessories

<http://www.zooplus.co.uk/shop/birds/cage_accessories>

Macaw Diet and Food Links

Here is the recommended list of websites for you to choose from when buying seeds and parrot food for your pet.

United States Links:

Pet Mountain

<http://www.petmountain.com/searchx/0/0/1/1/?s=Macaws>

Harrison's Bird Food

<http://www.harrisonsbirdfoods.com/>

Nature Chest - Bird Food

<http://www.naturechest.com/bifoforinri.html>

Petco – Bird Food; Treats

<http://www.petco.com/shop/en/petcostore/bird/bird-food-and-treats>

Pet Supplies Plus

<http://www.petsuppliesplus.com/thumbnail/Bird/Food-Treats/c/2142/2162.uts>

That Pet Place – Bird Food Supplies

<http://www.thatpetplace.com/bird-supplies/bird-food#!bird-food>

Great Britain Links:

Parrot Essentials UK – Vitamins and Minerals for birds

<http://www.parrotessentials.co.uk/vitamins-minerals/>

Scarletts Parrot Essentials UK – Bird Food

<http://www.scarlettsparrotessentials.co.uk/food>

Seapets – Bird Food

<https://www.seapets.co.uk/bird-supplies/bird-food/bird-seeds>

ZooPlus

<http://www.zooplus.co.uk/shop/birds/bird_food/parrot>

Bird Food UK

<http://www.birdfood.co.uk/ctrl/node:114;page:2;/bird_food
s>

Ideal Price UK

<http://www.idealprice.co.uk/compare.html?q=macaw-
food&ort=Bird-Macaw-Food-Sale>

Northern Parrots – Parrot Treatments

<http://www.northernparrots.com/treatments-and-cures-
dept139/>

Index

E

F

G

H

I

L

M

Photo Credits

Page 1 Photo by user Kaz via Pixabay.com, <https://pixabay.com/en/macaw-parrot-bird-hybrid-red-943228//>

Page 6 Photo by user Pexels via Pixabay.com, <https://pixabay.com/en/nature-animals-zoo-birds-tropical-1281689/>

Page 7 Photo by user Kayuli via Pixabay.com, <https://pixabay.com/en/parrot-ave-animals-macaw-850593/>

Page 9 Photo by user JD Mcginley via Pixabay.com, <https://pixabay.com/en/parrot-yellow-african-parrot-bird-177390/>

Page 13 Photo by user Joey Batt via Pixabay.com, <https://pixabay.com/en/parrots-birds-nature-animal-color-1438063/>

Page 36 Photo by user Anowa via Pixabay.com, <https://pixabay.com/en/parrots-bird-animal-macaw-948767/>

Page 38 Photo by user Dezalb via Pixabay.com, <https://pixabay.com/en/bangkok-parrots-macaws-yellow-blue-1151954/>

Page 45 Photo by user Nadine Doerle via Pixabay.com, <https://pixabay.com/en/parrot-ara-rainbow-parrot-bird-1182931/>

Page 49 Photo by user Luicampi0 via Pixabay.com, <https://pixabay.com/en/birds-macaw-tropical-bird-animal-651374/>

Page 74 Photo by user Hugo Hiram via Pixabay.com, <https://pixabay.com/en/macaw-parrot-exotic-bird-cage-zoo-508247/>

Page 82 Photo by user Condesign via Pixabay.com, <https://pixabay.com/en/ara-parrot-scarlet-macaw-bird-856574/>

Page 98 Photo by user JD Mcginley via Pixabay.com, <https://pixabay.com/en/parrot-yellow-african-parrot-bird-177390/>

Page 101 Photo by Purio via Rio.Wikia.com, <http://rio.wikia.com/wiki/Spix's_Macaw>

Page 108 Photo by user Kuszapro via Pixabay.com, <https://pixabay.com/en/macaw-parrot-bird-pet-wildlife-410144/>

Page 126 Photo by WikimediaImages via Pixabay.com, <https://pixabay.com/en/ara-hybrid-parrot-bird-animal-883762/>

Page 133 Photo by user Joel Fotos via Pixabay.com, <https://pixabay.com/en/macaws-in-the-natural-background-1200083/>

References

"Ara Macao" AnimalDiversity.org
<http://animaldiversity.org/accounts/Ara_macao/>

"Breeding Large Macaws" by Rosemary Low
Parrot Society Magazine in December 1999 (Volume XXXIII)
Pages 406-11.
<http://www.bluemacaws.org/en-gb/article/breeding-large-macaws>

"Breeding Macaw Basics" by Joanne Abramson
<http://www.upatsix.com/fyi/breeding_macws.htm>

"Bringing Pet Birds into UK" Jamescargo.com
<http://www.jamescargo.com/livestock_transport/PetBirdImport.htm>

"Macaw" Newworldencyclopedia.org
<http://www.newworldencyclopedia.org/entry/Macaw>

"Macaws-Breeding" Petparrots101.com
<http://www.petparrots101.com/macaws-breeding.asp>

"Macaw Facts" A-Z.com
<http://a-z-animals.com/animals/macaw/>

"Macaw Family" ParrotFiles.com
<http://parrotfiles.com/category/macaw-family/51>

"Macaw Types: Large Macaws, Mini Macaws, Hybrid Macaws" Animal-World.com
<http://animal-world.com/encyclo/birds/macaws/macaws.htm>

"Macaw Species" BeautyofBirds.com
<https://www.beautyofbirds.com/macawspecies.html>

UK Breeders Listings
<http://www.preloved.co.uk/>

USA Breeders Listings
<http://www.birdbreeders.com/>

Feeding Baby
Cynthia Cherry
978-1941070000

Axolotl
Lolly Brown
978-0989658430

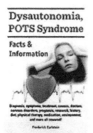

Dysautonomia, POTS
Syndrome
Frederick Earlstein
978-0989658485

Degenerative Disc
Disease Explained
Frederick Earlstein
978-0989658485

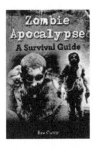

Sinusitis, Hay Fever,
Allergic Rhinitis Explained
Frederick Earlstein
978-1941070024

Wicca
Riley Star
978-1941070130

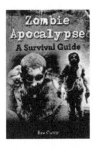

Zombie Apocalypse
Rex Cutty
978-1941070154

Capybara
Lolly Brown
978-1941070062

Eels As Pets
Lolly Brown
978-1941070167

Scabies and Lice Explained
Frederick Earlstein
978-1941070017

Saltwater Fish As Pets
Lolly Brown
978-0989658461

Torticollis Explained
Frederick Earlstein
978-1941070055

Kennel Cough
Lolly Brown
978-0989658409

Physiotherapist, Physical
Therapist
Christopher Wright
978-0989658492

Rats, Mice, and Dormice
As Pets
Lolly Brown
978-1941070079

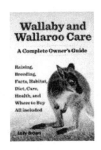

Wallaby and Wallaroo Care
Lolly Brown
978-1941070031

Bodybuilding Supplements
Explained
Jon Shelton
978-1941070239

Demonology
Riley Star
978-19401070314

Pigeon Racing
Lolly Brown
978-1941070307

Dwarf Hamster
Lolly Brown
978-1941070390

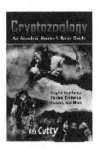

Cryptozoology
Rex Cutty
978-1941070406

Eye Strain
Frederick Earlstein
978-1941070369

Inez The Miniature Elephant
Asher Ray
978-1941070353

Vampire Apocalypse
Rex Cutty
978-1941070321

Made in the USA
Coppell, TX
27 February 2020

16269435R10095